D0615377

**BLACKBEARD'S CUP
AND STORIES OF
THE OUTER BANKS**

MErry CHRISTMAS

TO CAthy & JERRY !

© HRISTMAS ~ 1989

BLACKBEARD'S CUP AND STORIES OF THE OUTER BANKS

Charles Harry Whedbee

John F. Blair, Publisher
Winston-Salem, North Carolina

Library of Congress Cataloging-in-Publication Data

Whedbee, Charles Harry.
    Blackbeard's cup and stories of the Outer Banks /
Charles Harry Whedbee.
        p.   cm.
    ISBN 0-89587-070-3
    1. Tales—North Carolina—Outer Banks.   2. Legends—
North Carolina—Outer Banks.   3. Teach, Edward,
d. 1718—Legends.
    I. Title.
GR110.N8W48   1989
398.2′ 09756′ 1—dc20
                                                89-32193
                                                CIP

To the men of the United States Life Saving Service and the United States Coast Guard, all of whom have meant so much to so many helpless people

Contents

Foreword

THIS LITTLE BOOK is number five in a series of short stories from and about North Carolina's Outer Banks. Some of the narratives are historical fact. Others are legends handed down through generations as fact. Some are pure fantasy. These last were born of the long and often gale-ridden winter nights when the Outer Bankers were stormbound ashore and their offspring clamored for a story of long ago.

A critic, reviewing the fourth of these books, asked, "Will the well never run dry?" God forbid! So long as there are still Bankers who remember their glorious heritage and pass it on to their descendants in stories that cry to be written down or as long as there remain coastal fantasy and custom worthy of being preserved, the well will not run dry.

The ancient Chinese had a saying, "it is written." This, of course, implied respect for the written or printed word as being particularly reliable or worthwhile. Perhaps these books are a manifestation of that idea in reverse. Maybe some of these are stories that deserve to be written, made permanent, and forever available so that they may not be lost by the attrition of time and human frailty.

Anyway, enjoy these for their own sakes. Remember, a very wise man once said that legend is the true mother of history. A nation, a region, a person should not forget their antecedents.

> *From ghoulies and ghosties*
> *And long leggite beasties*
> *And things that go bump in the night*
> *Good Lord, deliver us!*
> *God bless you.*

Charles Harry Whedbee
Whalebone Junction
Nag's Head, North Carolina

**BLACKBEARD'S CUP
AND STORIES OF
THE OUTER BANKS**

The Guns of Vandemere

THREE APPARENTLY UNRELATED PHENOMENA in and over the waters of eastern North Carolina continue to puzzle and mystify scientists. They have done so for scores of years. Scientists see no connection between these occurrences and have no explanations for them other than a few unsubstantiated theories.

Phenomenon Number One. Several times each summer, always during daylight hours but never on Sundays, there occurs a series of loud noises that sound exactly like cannon firing. Heard from Vandemere southward, the noise rattles the windows of houses and causes newcomers to call the sheriff's office and even the Coast Guard to inquire as to the source. It is not thunder. It is not blasting of any kind. It is described by veteran sailors of World War II as sounding exactly like the noise from the firing of naval cannon. Even as far south as Fort Fisher people hear the noise and feel the tremors. It has been going on so long that they have even nicknamed it. They call it the "Seneca Guns."

A well-known geologist, Victor Zullo, of the University of North Carolina at Chapel Hill, has been quoted as saying that he believes it to be gunfire from navy ships offshore. This, in spite of the fact that the navy not only denies such firing but also the presence of any gunboat in the area at the time of most of the explosions. Dr. Zullo apparently believes that the navy, for reasons of its own, just does not want to confirm such firings.

Several knowledgeable people contend that it is the sound of the continental shelf breaking off at its edge and falling down into the deeps offshore. Geologists tell us that this simply cannot be true. The continental shelf has been thoroughly explored by divers in this area and they have found that it is a gently sloping underwater plain with no edge to break off.

Still others maintain that the noise is that of jet planes breaking the sound barrier. There is no way that this can be true. The noise has been recurring now for almost two hundred years, since a time when there were no airplanes, much less the ability to break the sound barrier. The rumbling roar continues intermittently for only about one hour and then ceases altogether. Generations of coastal people have noticed it and taken it for granted as just another fact of life.

Phenomenon Number Two. This mystery revolves around the charming little town of Vandemere, which was for many years entirely dependent on the seafood that came from the adjacent waters. It was a fishing village and a very productive one. To this day fishing and clamming and crabbing and oystering and scalloping are favorite occupations of many of its people. They were bred to the water and to following the water and they still love it. The unexplained noise which sounds like naval gunfire is clearly heard in Vandemere, and when it begins, the older natives and some of the young ones begin frenzied preparations for an easy harvest.

"Crab walk!" they exclaim to their neighbors. Or they shout, "Time of Jubilee!" or "Fish Walk!" They then rush down to the shoreline with buckets and baskets and even shopping bags along with rakes and shovels and even tongs. For they know that when the noise starts, for some reason unknown to them, the shallow waters next to the shore become alive with seafood. First the small fish and minnows seem to be making a grunionlike rush for the dry shore. Then the larger fish follow and thrash about in the shallows. The crabs come scuttling into ankle-deep water, and even the scallops sometimes jet into the shallow waters like tiny torpedoes. Only for one hour does this strange "crab walk" last. During that hour, however, the alert harvesters reap baskets and boxes and hampers of the sea's bounty. Then the noise comes to an abrupt halt and the harvest ceases. The "Time of Jubilee" is, indeed, a time of unparalleled abundance. Delicious seafood almost for the asking!

Lack of oxygen, say the scientists. The sea creatures are driven to shallow water in a desperate search for the oxygen they must have to live. Like goldfish rising to the surface of a home aquarium when the water gets too stale. But why only around Vandemere? Why only when the cannonlike noise is present, only to stop abruptly when the noise ceases? But most residents of the region don't worry about scientific reasoning. They are just grateful for the bounty and are glad to welcome the "Time of Jubilee."

Phenomenon Number Three. Some ten miles south of Vandemere (but a little farther than that if you go by boat down the Bay River, out around Maw Point Shoal, and then up the broad Neuse River), lies the equally charming waterfront community of Oriental. Much more extensively developed, it still has its roots in colonial Carolina and the waterborne traffic of that day and age. Sleek yachts and expensive waterfront homes now grace the town but, here and there, you can still catch a whiff of history and feel that you are going back in time to a more leisurely day.

There are modern farms nearby, too, and one of these is located quite near the town. It is rich and productive land and the portion of it that lies between Smith Creek and Green Creek fronting the Neuse River is particularly beautiful. It has not yet felt the hand of the developer, and most of it is just like the Almighty made it. It is here that our third phenomenon occurs.

Precisely at midnight every twenty-second day of November and at no other time there appears, near a huge gnarled oak on the banks of the Neuse, a ghostly light that sways and dances on the riverside. Back and forth, back and forth it goes, but it always disappears when approached. There is a sound of soft sobbing usually associated with its appearance but, after one brief hour, it vanishes and is not seen again for a year. Swamp gas, say the scientists. But in November? And vanishing when it is approached? And not seen again for exactly one year? And swamp gas making a soft, sobbing sound? The longtime resident locals just don't believe it. That light has been there every year for a long, long time and, frankly, they have grown quite fond of it. It is theirs. It is their own unique happening.

The ancients, the really old locals, the "been heres" as distinguished from the "come heres," believe that the strange happenings are indeed related. They think they are the recurring parts of a single drama that was played out many years ago. Understandably, they are very reluctant to talk about it except among themselves and then only in quiet, hushed tones. A new resident or a stranger has very little chance of ever hearing the tale and a newcomer, none at all.

The stage they set is in the early 1700s, when Sir Edward Moseley over in Edenton was already calling for freedom from the tyranny of the English crown, when the contra forces were plotting to have the colony taken away from the Lords Proprietors and made an official crown colony like Virginia and South Carolina so that a break could be made more easily.

Edward Teach, alias Edward Drummond, alias Edward Thatch, alias Blackbeard the pirate, was in his heyday and the so-called golden age of piracy was in full blast in coastal Carolina. The pirate was an exceptional fellow, to say the very least. He would probably have been a success in any line of endeavor he chose. As a pirate, he was a tremendous success, if any thief can be called a success. He was a very able seaman and navigator, an absolutely fearless combatant in hand-to-hand battle, and a superb organizer and leader of men. All this in a walk of life in which it was supremely difficult to impose organization and discipline.

More, he was many years ahead of his time in the use of psychology. He created an image of himself by his dress and his deeds and his imposing physical stature that struck terror in the hearts of his victims or would-be mutineers. He was a consummate actor with the utmost confidence in himself. Cruel he was, yes, and bawdy and rough and ruthless, but there was a side to his character that was as amazing as it was contradictory. He was a pushover for a pretty woman.

There must have been a gentler side to him than he revealed to his crews because women found him attractive and almost irresistible. Of a very tall and extremely muscular build, his chest, neck, and head were covered with a mass of jet-black hair, the color of his usual costume. He must have cut quite a figure when he was sparking the ladies.

The records show that he married at least fourteen times with never a divorce and never a widowerhood. His last "official" marriage was to one Mary Ormond, of Bath Town, who was at the time about sixteen years old. The ceremony was performed by his friend Governor Eden in Bath late in the year 1718. Most of the other marriages were performed by his first mate, on board his own pirate vessel. The nuptials were the butt of many jokes by his pirate crew, who used to claim that they never knew whether they were going to a wedding or a hanging. He fell in and out of love almost with the changing of the tide. Apparently he was completely and sincerely in love with the current object of his affection each and every time he got "married." Usually it was love 'em, marry 'em, put 'em back ashore, and leave 'em.

After Teach had audaciously captured and blockaded the port city of Charleston, he decided to come ashore, avail himself of the king's pardon then offered, and enjoy the vast riches he had accumulated in his pirating career. This he did, purchasing a house in Bath Town and settling back to enjoy peace and tranquillity.

Remember, pirates were not held in low esteem then, particularly when they were ashore. Blackbeard (or Mr. Teach) was a very popular figure. There is no record of his ever committing a robbery ashore. He kept a very small sloop, which he sailed alone. This vessel, which was fitted out more like a luxurious yacht than a pirate craft, he sailed about the sounds and estuaries of eastern North Carolina. He visited the homes of the settlers there, always finding a welcome wherever he went. He was famous everywhere. He could behave as politely in someone's home as he could violently when boarding a victim's ship. In private homes he is said to have always conducted himself as a gentleman. Teach was generous to his hosts and always left them better off financially than they had been when he arrived. On many occasions he behaved like a one-man welfare department, and most of the people grew to love him and admire him as well as respect and fear him. He was one of a kind.

One beautiful sunlit afternoon the pirate was conning

his boat out of the broad reaches of Pamlico Sound and into the mouth of the mighty Neuse River on an aimless, relaxed sail. He had no destination in mind but, for no particular reason, he turned out of the Neuse and into the mouth of Bay River. On he sailed northwestward with a fair wind, then turned westward, just enjoying the passing scene and the responsiveness of his sailboat. Running into shallower water just off what is now known as Windmill Point, he was about to bring the boat about and head back for the Neuse when, in the shallows near the shore, he spied the most beautiful woman he thought he had ever seen in his life. She was knee-deep in the water and a large bucket floated near her side. In her hand she held a clam rake with which she gently probed the sandy bottom. Her full skirt was tucked up almost to her waist out of reach of the water. To the restless pirate she presented about the prettiest picture he could imagine.

Easing his small boat up close to her, he dropped his sail, lowered his small anchor, and simply gazed at her in frank admiration. She was very young and very beautiful, with dark red hair and blue eyes that could almost look right through you. She rested her chin on her rake handle and stared back at the handsome figure in the boat.

"And who might you be, my pretty child?" asked Blackbeard.

"Why, I be Martha Piver," replied the girl, "and I be clamming and soft-crabbing as well for my father, Moses Piver. I know who you be, mister," she continued. "You be the famous Mr. Blackbeard and I hope you come in peace. My father be a peaceful man."

Roaring with laughter, the pirate assured her that he did, indeed, come in peace, that it was not his custom to do battle with womenfolk.

The upshot of this chance meeting was that Teach was invited to the Piver home. As was the custom in those days he was invited to stay the night. He accepted and this pleased Moses Piver and his wife, who considered themselves quite honored to have such a famous guest. As usual during such visits, Teach behaved like the complete gentleman. He left the following morning, promising to return for a longer visit.

Return he did, time after time, to seek the company of the beautiful, red-haired young woman. Often they sailed about the region in the luxurious, small sloop and Blackbeard would regale her with tales of his exploits and deeds of derring-do. There was no doubt that they were madly in love with each other. The pirate even took her up the Neuse River to a spot he knew where, he confided to her, he had buried a large hoard of gold and silver plate, as well as many jewels. The site was beneath the branches of a strong, young, oak tree very near the river. They picnicked under that tree many times and Teach promised her that, as soon as he could conclude some business in Bath and up in Edenton, he would return for her and they would be married. He would build her a fine home at that very spot, he said, so that she could be near her parents. That home between Smith Creek and Green Creek on the Neuse River would be their permanent home and he would go pirating no more. Half the gold and silver and all the jewels would be hers, he vowed, as a wedding gift.

When he returned to claim her, he promised, he would be sailing his fighting ship. She would know of his coming because he would have his crew firing all his cannon, one by one, in a salute to their happiness. Claiming supernatural powers, he also promised that when she heard that cannon fire, all the creatures of the water world would come and play about her feet in the shallow water where he had first seen her and they would be hers and her family's to choose from as they wished. Extravagant promises, but they were very young and very much in love.

Well, Edward Teach sailed away and Martha Piver never saw him again. Much later she heard about his marriage in Bath to Mary Ormond and, still later, about his return to piracy and his beheading at Ocracoke on November 22, 1718. She never recovered from the double shock. Her young mind just could not grasp the perfidy of the man whom she had loved and trusted, nor the horror of the violence of his death. She convinced herself that all this must be false and that he would one day come back to claim her as he had promised. She did not live long after that but passed away peacefully in her bed one night as she lay sleeping, no doubt dreaming of the return of her lover. Her body is buried in the little cemetery near Vandemere.

Many old-timers maintain that her spirit did not die. They say that it is this spirit or ghost who plays and dances around that now huge oak on the Neuse waterfront between Green and Smith creeks near Oriental where, during her short life, Martha Piver had laughed and danced and dreamed of a life with her reformed pirate. That very oak has been called Blackbeard's Oak for generations. It is shown today on some maritime charts by that name. The guns, the ancients say, are the guns of the pirate seeking to return to his love, and the crab walk or "Time of Jubilee" is the fulfillment of his promise.

Somebody must believe this legend because many people have on many different occasions secretly tried to dig up the buried pirate treasure. The marks of their diggings are there. So far as is known, not one of these surreptitious and unwelcome visitors has ever found the treasure. If he has, he certainly has kept it a secret.

The Legend of the Pelican

THE BROWN PELICAN (*Pelicanus fuscus*) is making a strong comeback on the Outer Banks of North Carolina. Years ago, this large and interesting bird was present in huge flocks along our estuaries and beaches. The use of pesticides and the violation of many of its nesting sites reduced the number drastically until, finally, none at all was seen on our coasts. Recently, though, the ban on some of the more harmful of the chemicals and a more enlightened concept of the needs of this wonderful bird have resulted in an environment where, once again, it can prosper and multiply.

One of the very most interesting sea birds to watch, the pelican dives from improbable heights above the ocean to seize fish. The huge body, striking the surface of the sea from such a height, cracks like a rifle shot. One wonders why every bone in its body is not broken in such a dive.

At home in its nest it is equally fascinating. Laying two chalky white eggs, it is a devoted parent and raises its young with care. Both the male and the female of the species share the responsibility of bringing up junior. For many years there was a legend that the pelican fed its young with drops of blood from its own breast. It is now thought that a curious bloody secretion ejected from the mouth of the flamingo may have given rise to this belief, that bird having been mistaken for the "pelican of the wilderness."

Actually, the pelican's feeding is quite different. One of the familiar characteristics of this large bird is its huge beak with greatly extendable skin in its upper throat. Although this jaw looks quite strong, it is really very weak structurally and is used with caution. Upon striking the surface of the water, the pelican usually traps one or several small fish in that pouch, fish being the main staple of its diet.

Upon catching one, or usually more than one, of these tidbits, the pelican either swallows the fish, ejecting the water from the side of its bill, or retains its prey within the seawater in its beak and flies away home to its young. Once there, the wide-opened beak provides not only food for the young birds but also training in the art of pulling a fish from water, as the young seize the fish from the pouch like a child bobbing for apples. This skill will prove useful to the young bird when it begins to fly and hunt the waters for its own prey.

Pelicans have been known to sailors and coastal people since the beginning of recorded history. The American Indian regarded them with reverence and refused to harm them. Ancient seafarers thought them very special and would no more harm a pelican than an albatross. You remember the lines from "The Rime of the Ancient Mariner":

> At length, did cross an Albatross
> Through the fog it came;
> As if it had been a Christian soul,
> We hailed it in God's name.
>
> .   .   .   .   .   .
>
> 'God save thee, ancient Mariner!
> From the fiends, that plague thee thus!—
> Why look'st thou so?' With my cross-bow
> I shot the Albatross.—
>
> .   .   .   .   .   .
>
> And I had done a hellish thing,
> And it would work 'em woe:
> For all averred, I had killed the bird
> That made the breeze to blow.

> (Samuel Taylor Coleridge)

The same taboos applied to the pelican. Controlling the wind was just one of the ways this bird could cause the seaman woe if injured. An old legend which survives to this day tells us that there is a very good reason why it is extremely imprudent to harm a pelican.

One of the seaman's greatest fears was not so much death at sea, in itself. What was most feared was death at sea while still "unshriven" and without Christian burial.

This, they were sure, would condemn them to an eternity of being washed about on the ocean floor with souls tormented by an inability to find rest and peace. These were the souls who appeared so often as ghosts, haunting the living with their pitiful cries for peace, peace, peace. Have you ever stood alone on the deck of a gently rolling ship at sea and watched the fog roll in with mysterious shapes and forms and heard the soft groans from the ship beams under the stress of the waves?

The legend goes that, after centuries of being lost at sea with no hope of redemption, no chance to confess their sins and be forgiven, the lost souls petitioned the lord of the sea for some sort of relief from their plight.

The lord of the sea took pity on them and decreed that these souls of lost fishermen and other mariners be transformed into pelicans and, as such, they were to continue to fish, only this time they would use their large pouches, rather than traps or nets or lines, to catch fish. When each had caught enough fish to fill the hold of the ship in which he had been lost, he would be set free to find the rest and peace he so ardently desired. If any mortal harmed them, that person was to experience the worst possible luck for a full year. And if a man should kill one of these large ungainly birds, he was marked for some disaster soon thereafter.

This legend is an ancient one, preceding the discovery of North America by many years. And its endurance is easy to understand. Belief in the transmigration of the soul is much older than Christianity, and it seems logical that the soul of an unsaved fisherman could be changed into a bird which not only follows the sea but also lives by fishing.

Thus it is that this favorite among sea birds has come to be revered and secretly loved by our Outer Bankers. They know the legend and they know all too well the terror of the possibility of being lost at sea. The "escape hatch" offered by this ancient belief appeals to them. While they will not admit that they believe in such superstition, they still, in the main, will not harm nor permit others to harm these awkward competitors for the bounty of the seas.

Sometimes, when an especially daring pelican attempts to steal a fish from the conveyor belts carrying fish from the ship holds to the fish houses, they swear at the predator and may even throw something at him, but you will never see them harm the bird. There have even been cases, in the past as well as recently, of the waterman and the bird forming such a close friendship that the pelican actually permits itself to be stroked and petted. Of course, this is usually followed by the gift of a fresh fish, but what's a fish or two between friends? After all, they both make their living from the sea and share most of the same risks.

For we latter day visitors to the ocean strand, all we can do is watch in wonder as the pelicans fly, very gracefully (for them) in long, wavering lines, occasionally peeling off from the formation to smack into the ocean and snatch their food.

In admiration, we may join the antebellum doggerel writer to say:

What a wonderful bird is the pelican
His beak can hold more than his bellycan
He can hold in his beak
Enough for a week
'Though I can't see how in the hellican!

St. Elmo's Fire

NEARLY ALL SEAFARING MEN, both modern and ancient, are familiar with St. Elmo's fire. Most of our own Outer Bankers know it and respect it, but they do not fear it. In the wonderful fishing village of Wanchese in the southern end of Roanoke Island, there is even a business named St. Elmo's Crab Company.

Scientists tell us that this natural electrical phenomenon occurs as a series of bluish-green flashes only when the atmosphere becomes so charged with energy that it must be released between the air and the nearest object, as just before, during, or after an electrical storm. These brilliant, mysterious discharges are eerie enough to cause fright amongst the uninitiated but are thought to be completely harmless. Physically, that is. Most automobile owners have experienced the small but non-luminous jolts of what is commonly called "static electricity" when they slide briskly across the plastic seat covers of their cars. This is a scaled-down but invisible manifestation of the same phenomenon.

Well, that is what the scientists say. Seamen, however, while not contradicting the scientific approach, know a different reason for that strange, if natural, occurrence. This is the story, based partly on history, partly on religious tradition, and partly on legend, that they tell their children and their children's children on those bleak days when they are weather-bound ashore, unable to get to sea to ply their dangerous but soul-satisfying trade.

Not many years after the crucifixion of our Lord Jesus Christ in Jerusalem, there lived in one of the cities near the Holy Land a very devout man who went simply by the name of Elmo. He was a Christian, one of the early pioneers in spreading the gospel of his Savior throughout that region. He organized the church and went about preaching to the poor and downtrodden, and his church grew rapidly. His personal life mirrored his teachings, and the people grew to love and to trust him. He was made a bishop and honored as such by other Christian leaders in the Holy Land. Bishop Elmo was a tremendous force of good in the region.

One of his favorite places to visit and to preach was on the waterfront in his city of Antioch, now a city in southern Turkey but at that time the capital of ancient Syria. In that place he soon became known and loved by all the fishermen and sailors whom he encountered. He blessed their fleets of fishing boats and blessed the sailors and fishermen themselves. He often went out with them in their small craft and shared the dangers of the deep. He became known as the sailor's bishop or the fisherman's bishop. He spoke their language, he shared their dreams as well as their dangers, and was, in short, one of them.

Word of his activities spread to other ports and to other sailors, and his fame increased so tremendously that seafarers would travel to his city to receive his blessing and hear his teachings and then depart to spread the news of this holy man through even more distant lands.

So popular and famous did he become that Imperial Rome, then the ruler of the known world, began to notice his increasing influence and grew jealous, then fearful, lest this man, also, become a threat to Roman rule. Rome brooked no challenge, real or apparent, to its rule under penalty of torture and death.

Thus it was that, under direct orders from the emperor himself, a systematic program of persecution was instituted against Elmo and all his followers. Whereas before he had been tolerated and largely ignored by the civil authorities, he now became an object of official hatred. The persecutions that followed were just as savage and cruel as those perpetrated in Rome and elsewhere during those intolerant times.

Finally, he was seized by the Roman soldiers and, when he would not recant his beliefs and refused to deny his Lord, it was ordered that he be executed. Not only executed, but killed in such a manner that his followers would forever remember the horrible penalty to be expected if anyone, bishop or not, refused to ac-knowledge the temporal and spiritual supremacy of Rome. It was ordered that Bishop Elmo be bound with chains, soaked in a combustible material, and set afire.

The royal decree was carried out but even as his body was beginning to blaze, a band of courageous seamen, hearing of his torture, stormed the provincial palace, armed only with knives and belaying pins. Daring the might of the emperor, they seized the dying Elmo and took him off into one of their boats, his body still blazing with that peculiar greenish-blue flame. Smother it and douse it as they would, they could not put it out.

Elmo spoke with his would-be rescuers and promised them that from that day forward for all time, he would be their patron. That the very flames with which Rome had sought to destroy him should now serve as a warn-ing to them in time of impending danger or disaster or as a sign of his presence and his protection, depending on the way the fire was displayed.

And thus the tradition grew that, when sailors saw that strange fire aboard their boat, they took it as a por-tent of events to come, either ominous or favorable. If only one flame was seen, they believed that disaster threatened, but if at least two flames appeared at the same time, they knew they would enjoy good weather and freedom from danger. Furthermore, if a single flame appeared on the head of a mariner, that man had best make his peace with his Maker because his days were numbered.

This tradition has continued down to this very day. The masts and rigging of sailing merchant ships are less commonly seen today, but St. Elmo's fire can still be seen on the Loran and radar equipment atop modern boats and on the trawls and other gear of present-day craft. Few seamen will risk raising an arm overhead when such fire is near for fear of attracting that potentially fatal sign to his own body.

So, the sign of the sailor's patron saint can be an omen for good or an omen for bad, but it is believed by some that it had better be observed and respected. If pressed, they can give you some startling statistics supporting their beliefs. They can and, on rare occasions, do name names and dates and places and I, for one, am not going to argue with them.

This, then, is a greatly simplified version of the legend of St. Elmo which some sailors tell. Now, just how far does secular history go in support of this widely held belief?

First, there is no gainsaying the fact that St. Elmo's fire does occur. Too many men of all stations of life have seen it and experienced the sensation of rising hackles on the back of the neck for there to be any doubt of that.

That the flesh-and-blood man existed there also can be no doubt. He is mentioned with consistency in too many documented accounts of the period for there to be any skepticism. It is also a matter of record that he was, indeed, a martyr for his faith under the Roman Empire. According to the official Roman records, he was executed in a most horrible way. By order of Diocletian, Roman emperor from the year 284 A.D. to the year 305 A.D., he was first broken on the wheel and then rolled in pitch, which was ignited. Before he died he was flogged with an iron chain and tortured with a red-hot cuirass. And burning pitch does, indeed, give off a brilliant greenish-blue flame.

Further, his story records that Elmo, who was also known by the names of Erasmus, Rasmus, and Ermo, was bishop of the Christian faith in the capital of ancient Syria. Gregory the Great (A.D. 540-604 and Pope of Rome from 590 to 604) has written that St. Elmo's remains are preserved in Campagna in the city of Rome.

Many devout Roman Catholics revere St. Elmo as a saint and observe his "day" every June 2, the day of his martyrdom. He is also known as one of the "Fourteen Holy Helpers" prominent in Catholic tradition and, as such, he has also become a patron against cramps, colic, all intestinal troubles, and even of women in labor. All this in addition to being the patron saint of sailors and seafarers.

These are the factors pro and con. These are the historical facts, the legend, and the religious traditions. What do you think? Must "truth" always stop when history draws the veil? Is there something to be said for the cold historical background of most legends? Is respected religious tradition all allegory or is some of it the unwritten record of things that have been and are true to this day? In the words of Pontius Pilate, "What is truth?"

Questions such as these, of course, can lead to sleepless nights but this is just one of the things we shall surely understand "in the end."

So be it, but one thing is sure. If you are near the sea and happen to observe a peculiar greenish-blue light or flame playing about the rigging of a nearby boat or a boathouse or even a summer cottage, just be careful not to raise your arm and risk the chance of St. Elmo's fire jumping down to play about the end of your upraised hand.

If you don't understand it and accept it, don't mess with it!

Blackbeard's Cup

"THEY SAY" THAT YOU SHOULD NEVER tell a story in the first person. "They say" that it robs the story of some of its interest and that the teller limits himself unnecessarily. Well, "they" apparently have never heard of the popularity of true confession magazines and the appeal of the "I was there" approach. Anyway, there are some stories that cannot well be told in any other way.

The time was the very early nineteen-thirties, right in the middle of the late and unlamented "Great Depression." Nag's Head and the remainder of the Outer Banks were still the "best kept secret" in North Carolina. There were miles and miles of undeveloped beaches on both the sound and the ocean sides of the famous barrier reef, and the whole area was as close to being a modern-day

Garden of Eden as it could be. I was, at the time, a student in the law school at the University of North Carolina and already a veteran of nearly twenty summers of roaming and loving the Outer Banks.

Also in the same law school at the same time was a young man who shall be known here only as Jack to preserve his anonymity. He, also, was an habitué of this golden strand since childhood and was a member of one of the finest families in eastern North Carolina. At that time Jack was even more conversant with the legends of the region than I, particularly the regions around Ocracoke and Portsmouth Island. A lifelong friendship had grown between us, and we young blades spent countless happy and carefree days exploring these sands and drinking to the full the mystery and wonder of the area.

This was the picture on that happy August day when Jack came to me and said, "Charlie, I hope you've got ten dollars to spare because that will be your share of the cost of hiring a gas boat to take us to Ocracoke tomorrow as well as board and lodging for one night." I hadn't known we were going to Ocracoke at all, much less on the morrow but at that age in life, "theirs was not to reason why." After all, what was there to lose besides a lazy summer day? It put a tremendous dent in my pocketbook but I just happened to have that amount on hand so, without question, the deal was made and the trip planned. I had no idea what Jack had in mind, but a trip to Ocracoke was pleasant at any time and even then the price seemed a bargain.

Why not a car? In those days very few people could

afford a car, and most of the ones who were affluent enough to try the trip over land and inlet usually got stuck in the sand. The ferries were adequate for the traffic at the time, but such an undertaking was fraught with danger and delay and frequent calls to the Coast Guard for an overland rescue. No, a boat was slower sometimes but usually very pleasant and more dependable. Given the wind direction and force and the type and location of the clouds, you could estimate the time of your arrival at any given point on Albemarle or Pamlico sounds with fairly reasonable accuracy.

The next day dawned clear and mild, and an early departure from the long pier jutting out from Hollowell's store and Post Office into the sound was made with high spirits and keen anticipation. There was no shade or awning on the Dutch Net boat we had hired and no relief from the blazing August sun, but all the voyagers were young and strong and already tanned a deep mahogany, so it made little difference. After all, who knew what adventure might lie ahead? We had practically no money to spare, but we were young and almost disgustingly healthy and it was summer and we were at Nag's Head! The copious lunch we took along was consumed before the sun reached the zenith and the trip southward was without notable event. After we ate, we rescued some chicken bones from the drumsticks, threaded them onto hooks, attached a crab line we found in the boat, and trolled for bluefish. We caught a fairly nice mess of fish which we gave to our "skipper."

Ocracoke landfall was made well before dark, and the smooth water of Silver Lake beckoned us to a safe landing at the pier. The short walk to the Pamlico Inn was rewarded by the usual cordial welcome from the Gaskills and we settled in for supper.

After a bountiful seafood supper, we stepped out into the gathering dusk of a beautiful Ocracoke evening and breathed deeply of the soft, salty breeze which was coming in from the eastwards. Up to that point I had not known that there was any special purpose to our journey. Just a trip "down to Ocracoke" with all its nostalgic sights and sounds and smells was reason enough, not to mention the wonderful people who were part and parcel of it all. Pleasures were simple at that time and in that place but they were deep and soul satisfying. Even in those days it was like stepping back into history. That was part of the magic of Ocracoke.

"Come on," said Jack, "we don't want to be late." When I demanded to know where we were going, he said, "To the castle." "Are you crazy?" I asked. "Shell castle is out yonder in the middle of the sound and Jasper, our skipper, won't be back until tomorrow morning!" "Take it easy, Chuck," he replied. "There's more than one castle around here, and the one we're going to is Blackbeard's castle. Come on with me."

On we went down the picture-book streets of the town in the direction of Silver Lake. There were places where the branches of the trees met overhead, forming a sort of fragrant tunnel through which we walked. Jack apparently knew the way, and it seemed to me we walked a good while before we came to a large, white clapboard house with a sort of cupola or lookout tower on top, overlooking the waters of the sound. "This is it!"

whispered Jack. "Look alive now and do exactly as I do and we may see something very few people ever get to see."

Walking across the broad front porch, Jack knocked three times on the huge door with his clenched fist. The door swung slowly open, just enough for me to see a large, lantern-lit room and the silhouette of a tremendous, bearded man peering cautiously out of the cracked door. "What is it you want?" growled the giant. To my amazement, Jack immediately answered, "Death to Spotswood." The eyes of the bear flashed to me. "And you?" he asked. Flabbergasted, I stammered the same thing Jack had said or as close to it as I could manage. That, apparently, was some sort of password, because the heavy door swung open and we walked in. Only my unwillingness to leave Jack in such a spot prevented me from bolting for the door and back to the inn as fast as I could run.

The room we entered had obviously been used at one time as a dining room or banquet room. With high ceilings and beautiful wood paneling, its only furnishings now consisted of a very large oak table in the middle of the room surrounded by a number of rather modern-looking bentwood chairs. The only illumination came from a huge kerosene lantern placed in the middle of the table. Its soft, warm light revealed about a dozen of the biggest, toughest-looking men I had ever seen. Most of them were heavily bearded with flashing blue eyes, and every one of them spoke with that Elizabethan inflection so usual on this coast, which has been called "hoi toide talk."

As the first order of business, Jack and I were required to place our hands on a large Bible and to take a solemn oath that, under penalty of death, we would not reveal anything that went on in that room that night for thirty-five years. With a shiver of mixed anticipation and apprehension, I took the oath and settled back into one of the chairs near the table. Jack did likewise. The others in the room did not take the oath but they took similar seats and for a short while we heard nothing but the buzz of several different conversations.

All at once and as though on signal, an abrupt silence engulfed the room as a door at the far end swung slowly open and the bearded giant who had admitted us strode in, holding aloft a large, silver cup of a most peculiar shape. Handing it to the man at the head of the table, he sat down and the man holding the cup raised it ceiling-ward and in a deep resonant voice chanted, "Death to Spotswood!"—the same phrase that had gained us admission to the house. So saying, he took a long draught of the liquid in the cup and passed it to the man next to him, who did the same thing and said the same words. The cup then was passed from hand to hand around the table until it came to me. Thrusting the cup against my chest, my neighbor fixed me with a stare so fierce and so demanding that my knees began to quiver. Too afraid to do anything else, I lifted the cup as I had seen them do and, in the best voice I could muster, repeated the words. Lowering the cup, I drank a large swallow of the amber liquid. My mouth and throat burned as if on fire! I gagged and coughed and finally managed to swallow, while the eyes of all that group were upon me. The stuff had not seemed to bother them at all.

While the silver cup was in my hands and before I passed it to Jack, I noticed that it was of a very peculiar shape. Much larger than any drinking cup or chalice I had ever seen, it was nearly so large as a punch bowl and was relatively shallow for its width. At two places on its lip there were cup-shaped depressions in the edge about three inches apart, which sloped inward and made drinking from that side of the cup a little difficult. I had quickly discovered that the potion we were drinking was some of the strongest corn whiskey I had ever sampled. It had a kick like a Missouri mule and that first swallow almost floored me.

Well, the evening wore on and the cup made round after round of the huge table. Frankly, I was scared not to take my part in the goings on, but I took as small sips of the potent liquor as I thought I could get by with. After a few rounds of the table, the talk loosened up and became more informal, and that night I heard some of the wildest tales about Edward Teach, the pirate, you can imagine. By that time we were on a first-name basis, but I never once heard the surnames of any of those present.

Fairly early in the evening I was enlightened to the fact that the oblate spheroid shape of the cup was due to the cup's being the silver-plated skull of Blackbeard himself. I became a little queasy when it dawned on me that, if the cup was a skull, then the little dips in its lip had to be the eye sockets! Carved in rather rough Elizabethan letters around the outside of the cup were the words

"DETH TO SPOTSWOODE." Just how long the wild tales and the loving cup lasted I have no idea. Jack and I made the excuse that we needed to go outside to get some fresh air. Once outside, we made the best speed we could to our lodgings and an exhausted sleep.

Jasper was back with his gas boat bright and early the next morning, and we made our way northward to Nag's Head and a safe landing on the soundside. Little did we know that Blackbeard's castle and the Pamlico Inn and the Wahab house would be either destroyed or damaged beyond repair by the hurricane that struck Ocracoke in 1944, but such was to be the fate of these and several other well-known buildings on that historic island.

Afraid to discuss our adventure in front of Jasper, Jack and I waited until we were ashore before we started talking it out. We figured the oath did not forbid our discussing it with one another—only with nonpartici-pants. It turned out that Jack was almost as ignorant of what the strange affair meant and how it came to be as I was. A long-time "Banker" friend had given him the pass-word and told him when and where to show up if he wanted to see something he probably would never see again. Acting on the trusted word of that friend, Jack had led us into the adventure.

We had both heard many times that Blackbeard's sev-ered head had been coated with silver and made into a punch bowl and used by some Virginia families. We knew, of course, that the royal governor Spotswood, who had brought about Blackbeard's death, refused to return to England after his term of office expired be-cause he feared (and probably rightly) that Blackbeard's friends, the Brethren of the Coast, would learn of it, intercept him at sea, and avenge the death of their friend and leader.

We kept our oath, Jack and I. At least, I feel sure that he did and I know that I did. It has now been more than fifty years and I figure that I have done my part to keep their confidence. I can see no harm and no oath violation in disclosing this now. I don't even know whether any of the party who met that night is alive, but I do know that the castle is no longer there.

In the trials and tribulations of pursuing a career in the law, the memory of the schoolboy adventure almost faded from my memory. One day recently I was looking through some old books I had inherited and I came across Crecy's *Grandfather's Tales of North Carolina History*, which was written back in the eighteen hundreds and was published by Edwards and Broughton. The author, Richard Benbury Crecy, lived closer to Blackbeard's time than we do, and he had devoted a section to the pirate. A perusal of the book proved Crecy to be a very accurate and a very complete portrayer of the history of this state. In his chapter on Teach he writes:

> Teach had seventeen desperate men under him. Maynard had more than thirty. The engagement was desperate. By a feint, Maynard's men were sent below and Teach was made to believe that Maynard declined the fight and was about to surrender. When Teach saw this, he sailed to Maynard's ship to take possession of her. As soon as he boarded, Maynard ordered his men on deck and then it was a hand to hand fight,

> Maynard and Teach heading it with sabres. Teach was mortally wounded after he had wounded twenty of Maynard's men. After Maynard had captured Teach's sloop, he cut off his head, fastened it to his bowsprit and sailed up to Bath in Beaufort County, then Hyde.

No mention here of carrying the head back to Virginia! And remember, Bath was Blackbeard's hometown. A great majority of the people there were his friends, including Governor Eden. In fact, Eden had performed Blackbeard's marriage ceremony just weeks before when he took a local bride. Maybe the severed head did not go to Virginia after all! Maybe it was "rescued" by some of the many friends of the pirate, and maybe it was them or some local silversmith who fashioned it into a silver cup bearing the curse on Spotswood. Perhaps the account of a punch bowl being made from the skull was a garbled one. What human has ever had a skull big enough to be used as a punch bowl? Maybe that odd-shaped, shallow bowl from which I drank was, indeed, the genuine article. Remember the secrecy with which it had been displayed and remember the location. Was it really the skull-bowl? I had to find out.

From that day to this I have tried as opportunity arose to trace the whereabouts and ownership of the bowl. Twice I thought I was on the verge of finding it, once in Norfolk and once in Virginia Beach, only to have the trail go cold. Both times it was rumored to be the property of a very rich Virginia collector, but when I tried as discreetly as I could to find him, I ran into a solid wall of silence.

I have discussed this search with my internist, a medical man in whom I have the utmost confidence, and he also has become interested. He tells me that if I can obtain possession of the object for only a few hours, he will help me have it X-rayed to determine if, indeed, there is a human skull underlying the silver plating. Before I meet my Maker I would greatly like to determine whether the silver bowl from which I drank is truly the skull of the famous pirate. The only way I know to do this is to obtain the cup so that it may be X-rayed, even if I am supervised and even if it is a brief loan.

In one final effort to do exactly that, I make this offer. I will pay one thousand dollars in cash to the person who loans me the cup from which I drank and I promise I will keep it just long enough to have it X-rayed. I will post a bond for its safe return and I pledge never to reveal the name and/or the address of the owner. There is no chance of a counterfeit being run in on me. I held the cup in my hands and I drank from it and I shall immediately recognize it if I ever see it again. My friend Jack has long ago passed to his reward or I would certainly enlist his help in the search. Maybe, from where he is now, he already knows whether the cup is the genuine article, but I surely would like to know.

I surely would.

New Berne's Bleeding Arch

THE CITY OF NEW BERNE (now shortened to New Bern) is one of the most beautiful and historic cities in the South. Its citizens, as are the citizens of Edenton, Bath, and other coastal settlements, are blessed with a God-given sense of history. The magnificent restoration of Governor Tryon's colonial palace is a perfect example of the reverence these people feel for their Swiss-American heritage.

Named after the city of Berne in Switzerland, New Berne was settled by Baron DeGraffenreid and the Palatines, artisans from Switzerland and Germany, in the late 1600s under the aegis of England. From that early date until today, it has played a prominent part in the history of North Carolina, some of which is known and some of which, unfortunately, can only be surmised. Situated at the junction of the Neuse and Trent rivers, New Berne was very accessible to the sailing ships of the day. It was, indeed, a deep water outpost in the new continent. So ancient is a part of the town that the framework of the original Anglican Church is still preserved there. In this early house of worship the dead were buried beneath the floor of the nave of the church to keep the Indians from knowing of any weakening of the town's strength.

On Queen Street, also in the heart of the "old town" of New Berne, one can still find a very old cemetery called Cedar Grove Cemetery. Commanding a beautiful view of the broad sweep of the Neuse River, this truly ante-many-bellum burying ground is the location of many fascinating legends and stories. Some of these appear to have real elements of truth, while others are apparently pure folk legend and may have sprung from some historical event.

The cemetery was conveyed in the year 1800 to Christ Church. The church itself was already an ancient landmark at that time, although it was in beautiful condition (it still is and used daily by its Episcopal congregation down to this good hour). Christ Church "opened" the cemetery in that same year and it has been in use, with many enlargements, to the present.

The old part of Cedar Grove Cemetery is enclosed by an equally ancient stone wall, and entrance is gained through a very imposing stone arch. The wall and the arch were constructed by local masons with large blocks of what the natives called "shell stone." This material, which is quarried locally, far from the distant mountains, is composed of millions of ossified sea shells and the fossilized skeletons of other large and small sea creatures. These little beings sank to the bottom of the Atlantic Ocean, which at that time covered New Berne. Over millions of years, they gradually hardened into a sort of coral-like stone in which you can clearly see the outlines of the sea shells. This material is very hard, like stone, but it can be cut fairly easily into large blocks. The masons of that day used these blocks well in constructing with great skill and loving care both the wall and the imposing archway of the entrance.

The cemetery itself is unusual and historic, but it is also marked by a fascinating phenomenon. Since the memory of man runneth not to the contrary, the archway has been used as the entrance for funeral processions into the burial ground. Its generous width provides plenty of room for the casket and the pallbearers on either side. From that day to this, such processions are greeted by the dripping of what appears to be blood upon the mourners passing beneath the arch. Not a stream, mind you, but a slow and temporary drip, drip, drip and then a halt. This substance is red, it is slightly sticky, there is no apparent source, and it always drops on funerals in a sequence of three drops, then a pause, then three more drops, then another pause, and so on.

One of the legends concerning this arch, held with conviction by some of the older residents, states that if one or more of the drops fall upon the head of one of the pallbearers, that person will be the next out of that group to die and be carried through that same arch.

They even quote some rather startling statistics to prove their point, giving names and dates!

There are other stories relating to the arch and at least one of them is based on the early history of this country. It concerns a duel that should never have happened and a tragedy that resulted in a great loss to North Carolina and to the nation.

New Berne produced many stalwart sons who played important parts in the early history of the region. The Baron DeGraffenreid, although Swiss by birth, was certainly a New Bernian, as was John Lawson, the Surveyor General of the Crown Colony, and Governor Eden, along with many, many others. One of the more well-known was a man named Richard Dobbs Speight. He was very active in the formation not only of Carolina but also of the nation. He was one of the first governors of the state of North Carolina, and he devoted his entire life to serving his region, his state, and his fledgling nation. He practiced law in New Berne when he was not holding some public office. He was widely known and loved by almost everyone.

Politics being what they are (and ever have been), Governor Speight in 1802 became embroiled in a spirited difference of political philosophy with a man named John Stanly, another New Bernian of some importance. He was a lawyer of considerable ability and was noted, most of all, for his fortes of invective and sarcasm. In his later years he was elected to the State Legislature, where he served with distinction. He served as Speaker of the House and ruled that chamber with a rod of iron.

The story is told that, when General Lafayette visited

the new United States in 1825, Stanly introduced a bill to appropriate considerable money with which to give the general an appropriate North Carolina welcome. He was bitterly opposed on this bill by a number of conservative members, and it was thought that the vote would be a close one. When the vote was called for, Stanly arose from his Speaker's seat, called another member to preside in his stead, and then, glaring down at his opponents, roared: "Mr. Speaker, I, too, desire to put every member on record so that if any one votes against this bill he may be gibbeted high up on the pillory of infamy." Strong language, even for those days, and words that could have easily led to a challenge to a duel. It is recorded that every man, somewhat awed, voted "Aye" and the bill passed unanimously. Such was the ability and the temperament of Governor Speight's adversary.

The debate in New Berne between John Stanly and Governor Speight grew acrimonious and, in the fashion of the day, it was proposed that the difference be settled by a duel to the death. Thus, a challenge was issued and accepted and arrangements were made for the "field of honor," in which marksmanship and luck would be called upon to decide who was right and who was wrong.

It was to be pistols at an agreed distance and firing upon signal. Speight was a man of peace and was unused to using a firearm, but his honor demanded that he abide by the rules and seek to kill or be killed by his fellow lawyer. It seems incredible today that men of the intelligence of those involved should engage in such illogical behavior, but dueling according to a strict *code duello* was the order of the day and the two men were locked into the situation.

Thus it was that the "field of honor" was chosen, set up, and prepared by the "seconds" of each man. The location of the encounter was chosen—a very pleasant alley paved with handmade brick and situated just a few hundred yards from Cedar Grove Cemetery.

There, very early on the morning of September 5, both Stanly and Speight showed up dressed in their very best clothing. Each was accompanied by a second. There were a few other witnesses there, too, some of them sensation seekers but most of them deeply concerned citizens. These very earnest men pleaded with the principals to call off the duel and find some other way to settle their differences. Speight might have agreed to this if an honorable way could have been found, but it is said that Stanly seemed thirsty for blood and that he cut short this discussion of alternatives.

The seconds then brought forward a brace, or pair of pistols, in a mahogany, velvet-lined case. The weapons looked and probably were identical, and each was loaded with the same amount of powder and the same size shot. The principals were then each shown the exact spot on which to stand so that the rising sun would be in neither man's eyes and were told to await the signal. Speight and Stanly each took his weapon, glanced at it, and then walked slowly and deliberately to his assigned station. The early morning sun was beginning to light the tops of the trees and a few birds began to greet the dawn of a beautiful, early fall day with song. Down on the field of honor there was a deathly silence.

Off to one side from the intended line of fire the seconds and the spectators waited as the elder of the seconds held aloft his white, silk handkerchief.

"Gentlemen," he said, "I shall now count to three. At the count of three, I shall release this handkerchief and you may fire at will. You do not have to wait until the handkerchief touches the ground but may fire at the count of three. And now, please take aim. One, two. . . ."

At the count of three, as the handkerchief fluttered downward, the two pistols roared as one. Strangely, both shots missed their mark and the duelists stood unharmed.

The pistols were reloaded and, once again, the two statesmen fired at each other. Once again they both missed! The spectators had grown in number as the firing continued, and now they redoubled their efforts to effect a compromise but things had apparently gone too far. Shots had been fired and under the *code duello* the whole thing could have been called off then with no shame to anyone, but this was not to be. This time, the two principals were placed ten steps apart facing away from each other. They were handed reloaded pistols and told to wheel and fire at the given word. It is thought that the seconds were trying to increase the likelihood of another miss and perhaps reduce the duel to an absurdity but, when the word was given, an entirely different result occurred. Whether intentionally or not, Governor Speight's bullet missed Stanly and imbedded itself in a brick wall. Stanly's bullet sped straight and true and struck Speight in the chest, inflicting a mortal wound from which he died in a very short time.

Thus, North Carolina was deprived of one of its brightest and most patriotic sons in the very prime of his life and at a time when his leadership was critically needed. Stanly, still bloodthirsty, soon thereafter tried to pick a quarrel with Speight's son with the avowed intention, it is said, of challenging the boy to a duel and thus ridding himself once and for all of not one but two of his opponents.

After the duel, it was first thought that Governor Speight would be buried in Cedar Grove Cemetery and it is said that a grave was opened there to receive his body. His family, however, decided that he should be buried on land owned by the family and located just west of the town of New Berne. It is there that his last resting place is preserved to this day.

Public indignation blazed against Stanly and there was talk of seeing to it that he was justly punished one way or another. He had abided by the *code duello* to the letter, however, and other than being shunned by many of his former friends, he was never brought to account for Speight's death.

There are those in New Berne who say that the majestic arch at Cedar Grove has not forgotten his death. They say that the drops of blood continue to call, even at this late day, for vengeance. Drip, drip, drip—avenge Speight's blood, drip, drip, drip—avenge Speight's blood. And those drops surely do look like blood and feel like blood to the touch.

Some explain them by surmising that the masons who constructed the stonework used notched iron spikes between the topmost stones of the arch—spikes which today are invisible to the naked eye because of the way they were embedded between the stones. They say that these iron spikes have continued to rust away over the years and that the moisture of rains, soaked up by the semiporous stone, supply the liquid that causes the arch to drip, drip, drip.

True it is that the arch does not bleed solely on the occasion of funerals—it bleeds at other times and at no predictable intervals. But it is also true that when it does bleed, it bleeds in groups of three consecutive drops, never more, never less, just as the seconds' count of "One, two, three" was in cadence at the duel and just as the slogan, "Avenge Speight's blood," is in the same cadence.

Whether or not you believe any of the legends associated with the ancient arch, it would seem to be the sensible thing to try to avoid being struck by the drops. The very least that can happen is that you may incur an expensive dry cleaning or laundry bill.

What do you think?

Horace and
the Coinjock Charade

SINCE LONG BEFORE THE WHITE MAN CAME to these shores, the area that is now known as Currituck County in northeastern North Carolina has been a sportsman's paradise. It was first populated by a people as hardy as they were adventurous, and their descendants have retained many of the finer qualities of their ancestors. Hunting and fishing skills were a part of the art of survival in the beginning, and these skills have been honed and refined until they have produced a crop of guides and hunting escorts unparalleled anywhere.

And they could not have had a more perfect land in which to practice their skills. The fields and woods were alive with wild game. There were wild turkeys, herds of deer, and vast flocks of ducks and geese, as well as

Carolina quail, pheasant, swans, loons, and, of course, uncounted millions of fish of all kinds.

Back several years ago, many of the heads of these families supplemented their cash incomes by acting as hosts and guides for sportsmen. To some extent the practice continues to the present.

Today most of the arable land has been converted to cropland and the local population has proven to be thrifty farmers and conservationists. Back in the late 1940s, they had achieved a wonderful balance of culti-vated fields and deep forests. That whole northeastern part of Currituck County was interlaced with rivers and bays and canals, and farther east the Atlantic Ocean beckoned with some of the best game fishing in the world. A paved highway ran straight and level past numerous well-kept and prosperous-looking planta-tions that bespoke the quietude and graciousness with which most of the people lived. It was a gentle time and a good time with plenty of leisure and opportunity to enjoy a good life with hunting and fishing to the heart's content.

The paved highway led all the way from the Pas-quotank County line down to Point Harbor and then on to the Outer Banks of North Carolina. The Intracoastal Waterway, that inland ship canal that affords safe passage for vessels up and down the coast, crosses the highway at the fine little town of Coinjock, where there was a drawbridge. The "draw" was of the ancient swinging type and was kept twenty-four hours a day by a resident bridge keeper and his wife. Normally the draw stayed

closed to allow vehicular traffic to cross the waterway.
The keeper would open it upon signal from the horn of
an approaching vessel and then close it again so that
traffic on the road could cross. This was operated by
hand by a capstan or treadmill going 'round and 'round
as it was pushed by the bridge keeper until powerful
gears opened or closed the bridge.

One of the beautiful homes fronting that highway was
owned by an elderly maiden lady whose name was Miss
Abigail Ambrose. She had inherited it from her father
and was very proud of her homeplace, which she called
Twin Cedars. Although she was in her eighties, Miss Ambrose managed the operation of her farm and employed
experienced overseers to cultivate it for her. Very inde-
pendent, she kept the books herself and gave general
directions and chose the order of rotation of her crops,
but the actual farming was done with hired help. Twin
Cedars was well equipped with modern farm machinery
and all the improved aids to agriculture that were available.

Miss Abby had extremely poor eyesight and depended heavily upon her spectacles to enable her not
only to read and write but to perform other chores that
needed detailed attention. She laughingly described herself as "blind as a bat" without her "specs" and she usually kept them attached to a long ribbon around her
neck. These and a silver-headed cane were her only con-
cessions to her advanced age. She had a telephone of the
old-fashioned "crank" type but she knew the "operator"
by name and got excellent service from her.

All the farm equipment at Twin Cedars was modern with one exception. That exception was Horace, her mule. As mules go, he was pretty well along in age but Miss Abby held on to him as a sort of keepsake of days gone by. He did not do any plowing or discing or other mulish jobs around the place, but he was well fed and was exercised regularly. He had a regular doctor in the form of a Dr. Liverman, an excellent veterinarian who had his office and clinic down the road in the town of Grandy, and who made house calls on occasion.

Liverman had other patients along that stretch of highway, too. Every farmhouse on both sides of the highway had at least one dog and most of them had two or three. The dogs were securely and comfortably housed either in individual dog houses in the yard or with comfortable beds under the houses near the foundations of the chimneys. These were mostly hunting dogs, foxhounds and coon dogs and rabbit hounds and deer dogs. They were trained to hunt different game but they had one trait in common. They all rejoiced in filling the skies with dog-music when they were on the trail of some quarry for their masters.

Miss Abigail had three of her own, two foxhounds and a beagle. They were able hunting dogs but mostly they were guardians of the manse. Riding to the hounds and fox hunting had traditionally been a favorite sport for past generations of Ambroses. One ancestor, Great Uncle Beauregard Ambrose, had been the local master of the hunt and was a rider of some renown. His scarlet fox-hunting coat still hung in a special place in the barn and his famous fox-hunt trumpet was housed there also.

A beautiful specimen of the trumpet maker's art, this custom-made horn was fashioned in strict accordance with the specifications of the old English horns. About as long as the average bugle, it was perfectly straight from the mouthpiece to the flaring "bell" at the other end. Made of some beautiful gold-colored metal, it was elaborately decorated with carvings of fox hunts and fox hunters and foxes and hounds. The inside of the bell was filigreed with intricate representations of flowering vines of some sort. One could not play a tune on it but, properly handled, it had a high, sweet, piercing note which carried for a great distance. Its call to the hunt was unmistakable. Of course, it had not been used for some time and was gathering dust on a shelf in the barn stable.

That stable had formerly housed several blooded horses commonly called Arabians. There was no Ambrose in residence now to ride them, so they were just another memory connected with that beautiful place. The stables did house Horace, the mule, a sentimental souvenir for Miss Abby.

This was the scene on one September night as a glorious full moon was beginning to rise in the east. Miss Abigail placed a telephone call to Dr. Liverman sometime around eleven o'clock. Holding down the "hook," she cranked the crank on the side of the phone and "rang up" the operator. Releasing the hook, she placed the horn-shaped receiver to her ear and heard a pleasant voice say, "Number pleaaz."

"Hello, Jelly," replied Miss Abby, "ring me up Dr. Liverman at his home, please. I know it's too late for him to be at his office."

"No, it's not, Miss Abby," responded Jelly. "I rang him for somebody else a few minutes ago and he's at his office right now. I'll ring him for you."

The phone on the other end of the line rang only once before a harried Dr. Liverman picked it up and growled, "Liverman's Hospital."

"Oh, Dr. Liverman," said the spinster, "I'm so glad I caught you. I'm worried about Horace. He just does not seem like he feels good and he won't half eat his food. He just stands there in his stall and looks bored. Will you please come out and look at him?"

"Now, listen, Miss Abby," replied the vet, "I was just out at your house two days ago to check on Horace and there's nothing much wrong with him. I have a hospital full of sick animals here and I just can't leave them right now. I may be up all night as it is. When I was over there Friday I gave him some medicine, a tonic, and I left a bottle of the tonic right there in the stable. Just give him all that's left in that bottle and he should be all right. Just take a funnel like you saw me do and put it in his mouth. Then pour the whole contents of the bottle into the funnel. That's all I would do if I was there."

"But, Dr. Liverman," wailed the old lady. "Horace has got such big teeth and I don't know how to put the funnel in his mouth and I'm afraid he'll bite me."

"Now, Miss Abby," replied the veterinarian soothingly, "you're a country girl and you're used to dealing with animals. Remember the time you helped me at calving time when your prize cow was having trouble? If you're afraid Horace will bite you, just take the funnel and go around to his other end and put the medicine in there. It will do him just as much good, anyway. Call me in the morning and let me know how you made out."

So saying, the good doctor hung up. Miss Abigail did likewise and shook her head slowly in despair.

"Funnel," she muttered to herself. "Other end of Horace. Give him the whole bottle."

Turning away from the telephone, she felt for her spectacles but they were not in their usual resting place. She fumbled around for several minutes trying to find the eye glasses with no luck. Mumbling to herself, she gave up the search and went on out to the barn and to Horace's stable. Looking everywhere for the funnel Dr. Liverman had used, she had no better luck. She was extremely dependent on her eye glasses and was searching more from familiarity with the stable than from eyesight.

Running her hand along one of the shelves, she touched Great Uncle Beauregard's trumpet and pulled it down into the light of her lantern. It was shaped like a funnel, all right, and she saw no harm in using it, so she gingerly inserted the mouthpiece into the toothless end of Horace. The mule didn't even open his eyes. It seemed like he had no inkling of what had just taken place and he stood as motionless as before.

Encouraged by her success, Miss Abby then felt along the shelf above Horace's head for the bottle of medicine the vet had left. She felt and she felt, but her hands could not find the bottle. Finally, standing on tiptoe, she reached to the very back of the shelf and there her hand felt a bottle—a pint bottle just like the one Dr. Liverman had used. In her farsightedness she could not read the word printed in bold letters across the front of the bottle: *Turpentine*. With trembling hands, she unscrewed the cap on the bottle, lifted the bell of the trumpet-funnel slightly, and poured the entire contents into the makeshift funnel!

The response was cataclysmic. Horace blared open his eyes, gave one mighty kick rearward, and bolted out of the barn and onto the paved road in the moonlight. With that full moon illuminating the entire countryside almost like day, Horace sped down the road to the east. As he ran the trumpet began emitting ear-splitting blasts. The noise filled the entire vault of heaven as he sped down the road.

Immediately, Miss Abigail's three dogs came tearing out of their houses, paws scratching wildly for traction as they pursued this ungodly noise. Down the road they went in full pursuit of Horace, giving voice to such canine howling and screeching as you have never heard. As they passed each farmhouse, lights came on in the bedrooms and heads poked out of upstairs windows. The foxhounds of the area, knowing full well what the sound of a horn like that meant, came speeding out of their kennels or out from under the houses, throwing clouds of dust behind them as they hastened to join the hunt and giving full voice to their delight at being summoned in the middle of the night to a hunt.

And thus the cavalcade grew. Each house furnished its contingent of excited, vocalizing dogs. True to their breeding, they gave voice to their delight and helped to fill the night with the sounds of the chase. The trumpet kept up its intermittent blowing, exciting the dogs to even louder howling, and causing even more lights to come on in the bedrooms of the homes they passed in their transit.

Down the road, in Coinjock, the bridge keeper heard the growing clamor. "Martha, Martha!" he called to his good wife. "Please come help me open the draw! There's a boat of some kind coming up the intracoastal and they must be in awful trouble the way they keep blowing for an opening!"

Racing out onto the drawbridge, they engaged the windlass and began to turn the capstan to open the draw just as fast as they could. The noise grew louder and louder, but they managed to have the draw wide open for the "boat" before they discovered that the noise was coming from the land, not the waterway. Too late then to try to close the draw. All they could do was stand aside and watch helplessly.

Down swept the cavalcade into the sleepy town of Coinjock with dogs howling and trumpet blowing continuing on the highway out, over, and into the deep waters of the inland waterway. All was confusion compounded for a few minutes, but the cold water must have had a sobering effect on the enthusiasm of the canine pack of the parade. All the dogs managed to swim out of the canal and, rather shamefacedly, trot back to their respective homes, none the worse for wear.

What happened to Horace and/or the trumpet is uncertain to this day. Divers went down in the waterway to investigate, but they found nothing. Later that day some boys while fishing found some disturbed reeds and some gouges on the canal bank which looked like some horse or mule might have climbed out at that spot. It is thought that Horace must have been able to swim and climb out after the cool water relieved his emergency. He never returned to the place of his treatment, although a stray mule was seen on occasion in the cornfields of the neighborhood.

The entire county either knew of or heard about the happenings and the bridge keeper was the heir of so many remarks that it went to his head. So famous did he become and so much publicity did he receive that he conceived the idea the next spring that he could be elected sheriff of the county. He paid his filing fee and ran for the office but it is a matter of public record that he received very few votes in the primary. One wag was heard to say at the polling place that anyone who couldn't tell the difference between a tugboat blowing for the draw and a mule in distress didn't have any business being sheriff.

The story of Horace is still told in Currituck County and, to this good day, when the hunting guides and fishermen are gathered around the pot-bellied stove in some filling station and they hear in the frosty night a high-pitched sound like the sound of Beauregard's trumpet, they will look at each other and say, "Well, there goes old Horace again. I hope he finds his way."

Ocracoke
—vs—
the King of Spain

THERE IS SOMETHING THAT LOOKS after the island of Ocracoke. Whatever it is, it does not prevent catastrophe, storm, heartache, or tragedy. Somehow, though, retribution is always made. Something happens that makes everything all right or almost so. This has happened time after time, as in the case of hurricanes that devastate but do not destroy the island, or shipwrecks that ultimately result in an enrichment of the people, or an isolation from the world that turns out, while it lasts, to be a priceless blessing.

It may be that the real underlying cause is the character of the people and their ability to stare disaster in the face and come up smiling. Also, these are devout, strong people like the Wahabs, the Austins, the Styrons, the

Boyettes, and many more. It just seems that Ocracokers have the ability and the will to survive, to hang on, to come back.

Case in point. In 1747 the continent of Europe was in turmoil. Spain, particularly, was beset from all sides, and things were not going at all well. His majesty, King Philip V, had managed to embroil Spain in a war with England and with Austria. This ended in 1713 with the Peace of Utrecht, but Spain thereby lost Gibraltar to the English as well as the island of Minorca. King Philip was also forced to enter into an *assento*, or contract, by which England was guaranteed a monopoly on the slave trade with the Spanish colonies, including the then-Spanish colony of Florida.

This so vexed the Spanish people that they broke the treaty, which led to yet another war with England in 1739. Philip V died on July 9, 1746, while the war was still raging and privateers of both nations were raiding the commercial vessels of the enemy. Philip was completely mad at the time of his death and the crown passed to a son, Ferdinand VI, who soon began to try to effect peace with England. The privateers continued their raids meanwhile. News was sparse and late in coming to the colonies in the New World. Sometimes this was the reason for the continuing raids and sometimes it was the excuse.

Thus it was that a Spanish fleet of privateers from the Spanish colony of St. Augustine in what is now Florida appeared off the North Carolina coast. Although peace had been signed between the warring nations, these privateers were ships of war manned by armed men who came mostly from the islands of Haiti and Barbados. The captains and the mates, of course, were Spanish but the crews and the boarding parties were as typical a group of cutthroats as you could imagine. They were on their favorite kind of venture, a raiding mission to destroy and pillage the English colonies, and this they did with a vengeance. They landed in the Cape Fear region, they landed on Core Banks, and they landed at Ocracoke Island.

Sailing through Ocracoke Inlet, they burned and sacked the boats they found there and confiscated their cargoes. Blackbeard, the pirate, had been killed and beheaded in that very harbor just a few years before, but the residents had not seen carnage like this. Storming ashore, the half-naked wild men burned houses and killed a number of Bankers who sought to defend their homes. They systematically slaughtered the livestock and carried the meat back aboard their privateers and did their best to just lay waste to the entire island. Similar depredations occurred at the other landings.

Having accomplished what they had set out to do, the men then hauled anchor and proceeded back to St. Augustine. Any resistance the islanders were able to offer was quickly silenced by the raiders, although it is recorded that a number of the visitors were killed on the island and in the waters of Pamlico Sound. Ironically, some of the very slaves whom England had been permitted to sell in Florida were used to pillage and kill English settlers on Ocracoke.

The citizens of Ocracoke were enraged. They had been promised protection by the Colonial Assembly even then sitting in Edenton but they had been given absolutely nothing with which to protect themselves. An angry delegation journeyed to Edenton and de-manded that something be done. Once again they were promised that a large fort would be constructed at Ocracoke and another at Cape Fear. It was promised that a formal protest would be made to Spain and reparations demanded. Money was actually appropriated by the as-sembly to build both forts but, other than a start on the proposed Cape Fear facility, nothing was ever done. Ocracokers were left to bury their dead and repair their damage as best they could. The opportunity to do the latter was not long in coming.

Ferdinand VI had been able to effect another peace with England but the super pirate, Sir Henry Morgan, was to ignore that "peace" just as the Spaniards had done. Sir Henry some time later led a flotilla of pirates to Panama City and looted that Spanish city. News of that incredible accomplishment was to be only the icing on the cake for the Ocracokers. Meanwhile they bided their time, although the memory of their losses continued to rankle.

So it came about that after peace had been declared and neither nation was supposed to commit any acts of war against the other, in 1750, just three years after the Spanish raid on Ocracoke, a tremendous hurricane struck the North Carolina coast. It just so happened that a fleet of five Spanish galleons carrying very valuable cargoes was lost off the coast. One was lost at Hatteras, another at Currituck Inlet to the north, a third at Drum Head Inlet in what is now Atlantic Township of Carteret

County, the fourth galleon near Topsail Inlet, and the fifth treasure ship on the shoals off the beach at Ocracoke Inlet!

This fifth vessel, named the *Nuestra Señora Guadalupe*, was under the command of Captain Don Juan Manuel de Bonilla and just happened to be the one that was loaded with more than one million solid silver "pieces of eight." Now, these Spanish coins, slightly larger than the present American silver dollar, were so named because they were somewhat soft and could be easily cut into eight equal pieces, thus "pieces of eight." The one-eighth, pie-sliced pieces were in common use as money at the time throughout the civilized world, as were the large, uncut, Spanish "tollars" from which they were cut. They exist today only in museums or in the collections of numismatists over the world and are highly prized as antiquities.

When the galleon was hard aground in the raging surf, the islanders, true to their heritage, rescued the captain and his entire crew at considerable risk to themselves but, realizing the entire operation was Spanish, that was all they would do and their helpfulness ended. The memory of the savage raid just three years before was too fresh, and they simply refused to help the captain salvage his silver cargo. Some even threatened to take the treasure by force as justly belonging to them but calmer heads prevailed and this did not materialize. The locals just smiled and shook their heads "no."

Captain Bonilla was no fool. He knew that his precious cargo was in a perilous situation, as he would be if he returned to Spain without this badly needed revenue.

He realized that one more good storm would break his wrecked ship into pieces in the surf and that all his pieces of eight would be lost in the shifting sands. As if that wasn't enough, most of his crew picked that time to mutiny. They just quit and refused to do anything. They argued among themselves as to whether they should seize the silver and try to escape to the West Indies but they, too, lacked any kind of transportation. Being un-armed, they did not care to tangle with the already hostile islanders, so the mutiny failed. The captain of the galleon was sitting on a powder keg and he knew it. Everywhere he turned, he found himself blocked.

Strangely, in the midst of this standoff, a number of the local citizens just turned up missing, including some of the most able seamen on the island. Nobody seemed to know where they were or what they were doing, but there was a mystifying lack of concern about their absence.

Just as strangely, a sloop appeared on the scene, sailing southward along the coast. On being hailed by Captain Bonilla, the sloop came up alongside very smartly and, at his invitation, her skipper boarded the wrecked ship. After explaining the situation, the Spanish captain was able to strike a bargain with the skipper of the sloop whereby that vessel's crew would off-load as many of the sacks of coins as the smaller vessel could safely carry and transport the cargo to a northern port for transshipment to Spain. The young skipper did not seem to mind at all when he was told that his payment for this service would have to wait to be approved by the royal government of Spain. The bargain having been agreed upon, the crew of the sloop worked with enthusiasm loading the silver coins aboard their vessel until it rode very deep in the water with scant freeboard to offer protection in case of a storm. The workers went about their task of loading the conveniently empty little craft, it is said, with broad smiles. They soon completed the transfer and the overloaded sloop handled very sluggishly.

Written history does not record it, but local tradition says that the sloop cast off from the wrecked Spaniard, headed south, and then came about to head north, with the freshening breeze almost dipping water on her leeward side. It is said (not written) that as the sloop came again alongside the *Nuestra Señora Guadalupe*, the helmsman steered almost dangerously close to the wreck. It is said that when this happened a crewman threw aboard a note wrapped around one of the pieces of eight. No one on board the wreck at that time could read the note as they knew no English. The man who picked it up thought it must be some sort of manifest or bill of lading for the silver. Anyway, it was placed in the captain's cabin awaiting his return from shore.

When that worthy arrived back on board, so the legend goes, he was enraged to find that the writing thrown from the sloop was not a bill of lading but a receipt which stated that the silver was "accepted" in partial payment for the depredations and murders of three years before. The receipt was addressed to the King of Spain and was signed simply, "God save the King"! The heavily laden sloop was nowhere to be seen either with naked eye or the ship's spyglass.

Written history does record that the Spanish captain,

in desperation, finally appealed to the civil authorities of the colony that his fellow countrymen had ravaged. The English authorities did respond. Before another storm could strike, Governor Johnson sent Colonel Innes to Ocracoke to take charge in the governor's name. An English man-of-war was then sent to the aid of the beleaguered captain. The remainder of the silver was transferred to the man-of-war along with the would-be mutinous crew members. These men were put in chains and charged with mutiny. The English vessel then proceeded to Spain with the silver, Captain Bonilla, and his first mate along with the mutineers. What finally became of the captain, his officers, or the mutineers is not known, but it is not hard to guess. These were the days of the Spanish Inquisition and human life was not held in very high regard.

Once again written history draws the veil here and we must go to the unwritten history, the traditions and folklore of the people. The strong impression is that the sloop, laden with silver coins to her gunwales, lay peacefully hidden in a remote cove behind Hatteras Island. It is said that the men took turns at guard duty and seeing to it that the sloop was bailed and properly secured. After the furor of events following the storm had calmed down, the colonial government found other things to worry about. They had never been too interested in the disappearance of the Spaniard's silver anyway.

Then, according to legend, the cargo was divided into shares of approximately equal value. Each member of the crew of the sloop took only one share for his efforts. The remainder of the easily negotiable haul was divided among the families of the people who had suffered most in the Spanish raid of 1747. The larger shares went to the families who had suffered the loss of a loved one, the smaller shares to the folk who had had boats burned and sunk, houses burned to the ground, farm animals destroyed, and crops ruined. It didn't amount to complete recompense, of course, but it helped and helped mightily.

No one ever mentions names but it is said that a good many of the fishing boats that were built soon thereafter were paid for in pieces of eight, as were several nice but simple houses and places of business. Of course, pieces of eight were in general circulation up in Edenton and in Bath so there is no reason on earth why payment in this common coin should excite suspicion or even comment in Ocracoke.

Once again, destruction and loss had come from the sea and from the sea had also come restoration and at least partial payment for loss. It has happened in the past, it continues to happen once in a while in the present, and the old timers seem to know that it will continue to happen on occasion in the future.

The True Story
of Rasmus Midgett

MOST MEN LEAD DRAB, RATHER BORING LIVES wedded to routine and responsibilities, both financial and physical, which life has imposed upon them. Some, like Walter Mitty, dream of being involved in high adventure and of performing heroic acts to the applause of all and sundry, only to be rudely awakened to the humdrum chores of meeting the monthly bills and responding to the demands made upon most of us every day.

Others there are who seem to be thrust into herculean action and almost superhuman achievement. Such men of heroic mold seem to loom larger than life and are of the material from which legends are made. Their every act seems charged with drama, and they attempt almost gargantuan deeds with the ultimate in courage and a complete dedication to duty and principle. These are the Sergeant Yorks, the Charles Lindberghs, the Albert Schweitzers of our time.

Such a man was the real-life hero, Rasmus Midgett. Born in the tiny village of Waves on Hatteras Island, Midgett had the advantages and the disadvantages of growing up in the late 1800s on one of the wildest and most beautiful coasts in the world, the Outer Banks of North Carolina. Somewhere back in his lineage the name Rasmus must have been given to an ancestor in honor of the patron saint of sailors, St. Elmo, who is also known by the names of Erasmus and Rasmus. This was the name given to the Hatteras boy and it seems there could not have been a more appropriate one.

Back in those days the United States maintained what was called the Life Saving Service, a forerunner of the United States Coast Guard. Its members lived in the Life Saving Stations scattered up and down the coast and, under the command of a captain or keeper, were charged with attempting to rescue those unfortunate individuals who were trapped aboard wrecked vessels on this "Graveyard of the Atlantic."

From the beginning Rasmus Midgett wanted with all his heart to be a member of that service and when he was finally accepted and put on the roster as a surfman, he began to exhibit unusual qualities, to say the least. Today it seems certain that he possessed to a remarkable degree what later came to be called extrasensory perception. Long before the advent of Professor Rhyne and his historic work with this phenomenon at Duke University, Rasmus Midgett was foretelling future events, particularly shipwrecks on the Outer Banks. Not always, mind you, but often enough that it became noticeable.

These precognitions came to him in dreams when he was fast asleep and, time after time, his dreams of forthcoming shipwrecks actually came to pass and in complete detail as he had foretold them. Midgett was devoted to his calling to rescue the perishing and, to him, it seemed only natural that he had been given such a gift. Time after time he would relate his dream and time after time the dream came true with frightening accuracy. He did not predict all such mishaps but those he did predict seemed to always occur.

In addition to being a devoted surfman, Midgett was also a man of tremendous courage. It almost seemed as though he knew that he could attempt apparently impossible deeds and come through unscathed.

We have seen that the duty of the Life Saving Service was exactly what the name implies. These brave men, no matter what the risk to themselves, were to use every effort to rescue the men aboard ships that had wrecked just offshore on the Outer Banks. There were several ways to attempt this. Each station was provided with a surfboat, a double-ended stout craft that was rowed by the surfmen out to the wreck if the surf was not so rough as to prevent the boat being launched through the waves. Later the service would have gasoline motors and self-bailing boats, but in the beginning it was row your way out through the surf and then try to get back to land with your rescued passengers and crew.

Sometimes the surf was just too rough to launch any kind of boat through that maelstrom. Oh, they tried.

Many a surfman has wound up with a broken arm or leg when the sea threw back the boat they were trying to launch. When the sea was this rough, there was an alternative method to try. Each station had what was called a Lyle gun. This was nothing more than a small, solid brass cannon about two or three feet in length which mounted on a sled. This gun was carried by beach cart to the shore opposite a wreck and then unloaded onto the sandy beach. First a powder charge in a cloth bag was inserted into the cannon and tamped down to the butt end of the gun. Then a projectile was loaded into the mouth of the cannon on top of the powder charge. This projectile was attached to a light but very strong line, and written on the projectile in several languages were instructions to the master of the wrecked vessel to carry the line just as high in his rigging as he could safely go and then haul away and pull it in. When this was done the skipper found the light line attached to a much heavier line, and that line to a block and pulley, from which two heavy lines ran back to the beach.

When this was made secure to the mast, the Life Saving crew on the beach could send out a ring buoy with a pair of stout, knee-length shorts attached. This was called a breeches buoy and a person could sit down inside the ring and inside the britches and be hauled safely to shore. The device would then be returned to the wreck time after time until all hands had been brought safely to the shore. After years of practice, the surfmen became adept at aiming the Lyle gun so that the light line would fall across the yardarms and rescue could be thus achieved. This was done when the wreck was close enough inshore for the power charge to discharge the projectile far enough to reach the wreck.

These were some of the things that were done when the station keeper and his crew were summoned to the scene of a wreck. Other duties of the surfmen consisted of a daily patrol, on foot or on horseback or ponyback, up and down the beaches both in fair weather and in foul to keep a lookout for vessels in distress. The patrol would usually go halfway to the next station and then return to make out a report.

But back to the surfman Midgett. Rasmus owned a marsh pony, or Outer Banks pony, whom he had named Gilbert and with whom he had formed a bond of mutual respect and love which was beautiful to behold. Gilbert was his own personal property and had never had another owner. Rasmus had tamed him from a creature as wild as a sand fiddler, and the two were very close. When it was Rasmus's turn to go on patrol, he always rode Gilbert. Without saddle, reins, or other impediments, he guided Gilbert by pressure from his knees, and the tough pony seemed to anticipate what Rasmus's next signal would be. This patrol duty, although lonely and sometimes dangerous, was part and parcel of the full duty of a surfman. What "full duty" meant to Rasmus became clear one wild and stormy night when the sea went mad under the force of the screaming wind, which was piling huge breakers ashore and driving a blinding rain in such a torrent that it almost prevented visibility.

Midgett happened to be stationed at the Gull Shoal Life Saving Station on that particular night. The other surfmen were laboring down the beach that night in an attempt to help two vessels in distress. It was Rasmus's turn to be on patrol, so he was sent off in the opposite direction to look for other distressed vessels.

Mounting his trusted marsh pony, Midgett urged him gently for miles up that storm-ravaged beach in the wild night. It must have seemed to Rasmus that he and his pony were the only living things outdoors on that hellish night, but they continued their patrol, ploddingly and steadily and always keeping a sharp lookout on the raging sea. Nothing was visible but turmoil and driving spume.

Then, very faintly but distinctly, he heard a human voice which seemed to be calling for help. The voice, incredibly, seemed to be that of a woman. Halting his pony, the surfman gazed long and intently at the ocean. He must have wondered if this could be an hallucination, born of his desire to serve and his strange extrasensory powers. At any rate, his station with all its lifesaving resources was far to the south. He had no equipment with him. No Lyle gun, no surfboard. Nothing but himself and his pony.

Urging Gilbert down closer to the edge of the sea and looking and listening intently, he finally saw a three-masted schooner breaking up in the heavy surf. Squinting his eyes, he could make out the figure of a woman holding a child and clinging to an already sagging rail. She it was who was screaming for help, and her position was so precarious that it seemed that she must be washed away with each succeeding wave.

It was against all precedent, contrary to all his surfman's training and his own instinct for self-survival, but Midgett urged his pony down into the raging surf. Gilbert turned his head and looked at his master as if to ask if Rasmus had gone completely crazy, but no, the steely eyes of the surfman's face showed all too well what he intended.

Out toward the breaking ship and the woman they went, Gilbert and Rasmus, the pony bracing as only a marsh pony could against the violent wave action. These ponies are famous for their sure-footedness and agility, and on this night it was a good thing that Gilbert was of that breed. Getting closer to the wreck, the surfman screamed to the woman to jump, hoping against hope that he could catch her as the waves bore her shoreward. Instead of jumping, the woman threw her child, a boy, into the raging waters.

Like a cornerback on a football team, Rasmus caught the boy solidly against his chest and wrapped both arms around him. Gilbert staggered and almost went down, but he was tough and he was sure-footed and he regained his balance in the shifting sand and carried his master and the boy back to the beach.

Placing the terrified and half-drowned boy on the beach, Midgett then rode Gilbert back into that raging surf and rescued the woman just as she lost her hold on the slippery and sagging rail of the ship. Once again, it was back to the beach and the woman was reunited with her son.

Incredibly, our surfman and his faithful mount went back through that treacherous surf not once more but nine more times, each time rescuing a person from the wrecked schooner, which by that time was dissolving in the waves. And as if that were not enough for even a superman to do, the heroic pair went back one final time and retrieved the bodies of three seamen who had died in the wreck!

Now, if you saw such a scenario in a movie, you would almost certainly scoff and say that such a thing just could not happen. But it did happen. And it happened just that way.

According to the official records, the name of the wrecked schooner was the *Priscilla* and her remains washed completely ashore the next day. The woman was placed aboard Gilbert with her son in her arms and the other survivors and Midgett walked with them back to the station. At Gull Shoal they were given dry clothing and a warm meal. Even as you read this account, three of the doors from the wrecked *Priscilla* are part of the ancient home of Rasmus Midgett and his wife in the little village of Waves on Hatteras Island.

In recognition of this incredible act of heroism, the United States Congress awarded Rasmus Midgett the gold lifesaving medal "in testimony of heroic deeds in Saving Life from the Perils of the Sea." In all of history, only eleven of these medals have been awarded. Today this one is the proud possession of Rasmus Midgett's descendants. Midgett and his devoted wife are buried on Hatteras Island just as he would have wanted it, in sound of the sea where he achieved his finest hour.

The tradition goes on. *Semper Paratus* (always prepared) is not only the motto of the United States Coast

Guard—it is also the credo and the inspiration of the men who, to this good day, do their utmost to protect and rescue "those in peril on the sea"!

Talk about tradition! Do you wonder that the Bankers are proud of their heritage?

The Cora Tree

DEEP IN THE HEART OF THE VIRGIN FOREST on Hatteras Island, there stands a gigantic live oak which botanists estimate must be at least a thousand years old. That, in itself, is not very remarkable. There are other live oaks in that forest, some of which almost certainly are as old. It is well known that such trees exist in virgin forests all the way from North Carolina to Louisiana where the rapacious hand of the timber cruiser has not destroyed them or the creeping development of subdivisions has not doomed them to destruction. Botanists have a saying that such trees "grow at least three hundred years, flourish at least three hundred years, and die at least three hundred years."

What is remarkable about this particular tree is what has happened to it. Down to the present day, the forest giant bears mute testimony to the trauma that it underwent some hundreds of years ago.

Extending from the very top of the huge trunk down to the root system there is a savage scar obviously left by a bolt of lightning, or something similar to a bolt of lightning. Also remarkable is the single word burned into the trunk at a point higher than a tall man's head. That one word is *CORA*, and it is burned, not carved, into the very heart of the live oak. The four letters are each about four inches high and about an inch deep through the bark of the tree. The charred wood from that burning is still there and will still smut the finger of the curious investigator today.

Hatterasmen are reluctant to talk. They prefer not to make common knowledge of the tales and legends that have been handed down to them for generations from grandfather to grandson as a sort of unwritten tradition or history of their beloved region. The ancients, or most of them, seem to know the story of the "Cora Tree." When they do talk, they all agree on the events that occasioned those strange marks. This is the story they tell.

Back in the early years when this region was being settled by their forebears, times were simple but hard. The people knew and trusted one another, and their very lives frequently depended on being able to trust and rely upon their neighbors. Everyone was dependent in those days upon Mother Sea not just for a living but also for sustenance itself. They were courageous people

and they were hardy and most of them were very rever-
ent. They shared what they had with each other, bore
each other's burdens, and partook of each other's joys
and sorrows. They were, indeed, a very close-knit band.
It was at that time almost like one great family. Some of
them were superstitious and some were extremely suspicious of strangers and outsiders. They had good cause
to be. Even today, if you listen carefully, you can hear the
distinction made between the "been heres" and the
"come heres."

Thus it was with some misgivings that they became
aware of a very unusual woman on the island. No one
seemed to know exactly when she came or from
whence, but she lived alone in a very crude hut in the
heart of the forest. Alone, that is, except for her "knee
baby," the small child who was her constant companion.
There was no man of the house. The hut had been abandoned prior to her coming, and no one knew or cared
who owned or claimed to own the wooded area where
it was located.

Remember, this was the time of the great witch hunts
in the northern settlements of this country. The Reverend Cotton Mather was in full cry in Massachusetts, and
the infamous Salem witch hunts were growing in savagery week by week. This same Pilgrim preacher, Reverend Mather, described the colonization of the eastern
seaboard of America in almost lyrical terms in his book
Wonders of the Invisible World. The Puritans, he declared, had populated what had been a desert inhabited
by devils. By devils, of course, he meant the native In-

dians whose savage rites he could only regard as having been ordained by Satan.

The Hatteras settlers had heard of these atrocities from visiting seamen who unloaded cargoes from their ships. They paid scant attention because these strange goings-on were happening many miles away and the locals were not by nature cruel people. There had been no witch hunting thereabouts and they wanted none. The Englishman, Eric Maple, in his beautifully researched volume *The Dark World of Witches*, published in 1962, offers a plausible explanation. "Legislation against witchcraft was actually introduced in Massachusetts in 1641," he states. "The Southern Colonies were relatively free from witch persecution because there, under Episcopalian rule, there was little of the bigotry of the north" (p. 181). Of course, there was no Puritanism in the South but instead a great deal of tolerance. Thus it was that the strange behavior of their new inhabitant was viewed with wonder and misgiving but not, initially, with any hostility.

Then strange things started to happen with increasing frequency. Even during the times when the skilled fishermen of the island could catch few fish, the "quare woman" always seemed to have an abundance of fresh fish. Then there was the time when one of the local little boys ran at the woman's baby and mocked it with hoots and yells. He stoutly maintained afterward that the infant snarled and spat at him like no baby he had ever seen. The very next day the little local fell seriously ill and almost died from a fever.

Cora, for that was the only name she was ever known by, usually walked with her head held high and the baby clutched to her breast. Once, when Cora was known to have touched a cow as she walked by it, the animal's milk dried up and it had to be sold by the owner.

Of course, none of these things could be directly attributed to Cora but it seemed strange that she had always been seen in the neighborhood just before misfortune struck. Then too, the child did not seem like a normal baby. It was never seen to smile but looked directly and fixedly at people with a knowing and seemingly calculating frown as though plotting something.

This was the scene and the atmosphere when the brig *Susan G.*, with Captain Eli Blood in command, ran hard aground on the Inner Shoal and began to break up in the heavy surf. Captain Blood and his crew of former slaves from Barbados labored manfully to save the cargo. Helped by the Hatteras residents, they went back and forth from the *Susan G.* to the beach, depositing in great piles what they were able to save. A northeast squall put an end to these salvage operations and the only thing left for the captain and his crew to do was to wait for word from the owners, which might take weeks in coming considering the unpredictability of communications of any kind.

The Hatterasmen were accustomed to men like the captain, they knew him as one of a type and his papers were all in order. Knowing this, they made him welcome in their homes as a brother mariner who had lost his ship. The crew was comfortable in tents they fashioned on the beach from the salvaged sails of the wreck. The weather had turned quite balmy and the only inconvenience they faced was boredom. Jack ashore misses the daily routine of manning and conning his ship and even the excitement of the frequent danger he must face afloat. From a period of enforced idleness, which the Barbados natives now had to endure, some sort of mischief should have been anticipated.

These Barbados islanders were steeped in the lore and beliefs of "black" witchcraft. On the beach they soon resorted to their age-old customs of "working roots" and other magical charms to ward off the powers of darkness. They devoutly and sincerely believed in witches and in the power of the Prince of Darkness to harm humans through witches.

Captain Eli himself was no less convinced of the existence of evil and supernatural powers with power of life and death over ordinary humans. Now, mind you, these feared creatures were "black witches," not to be confused with so-called "white witches" or "cunning men" who had the power to counteract and defeat the evil ones. The captain was a longtime resident of the village of Salem when not at sea, and he was quite familiar with the Reverend Cotton Mather and with the Reverend Increase Mather and with their crusades against the powers of darkness. He had read their books and studied their methods in detail. To tell the truth, Blood considered himself to be a white witch or "wizard" with God-given powers to search out and expose evil (black) witches and their "familiars," who were the unnatural servants of the witches and who, from time to time, assumed various shapes and forms such as frogs or cats or monkeys. This captain claimed to have familiars of his own whom he fed with drops of human blood and whose services he employed to help him in exposing the agents of darkness. He considered himself to be the mortal enemy of Satan, a man peculiarly endowed to conduct the battle against the agents of the evil ones. He sincerely believed this and his crew did also and they feared him.

And so it came to pass, inevitably perhaps, that Blood set himself to find out once and for all whether the strange woman the islanders described to him was, indeed, a black witch. If she was a witch, she should be exposed and exorcised before the Prince of Darkness compelled her to further harm these innocent fisher folk.

Having nothing else to do with his time, he set about his self-appointed tasks with determination and enthusiasm. His zeal knew no bounds. In his heart of hearts he did not entertain the slightest suspicion that Cora was not a genuine black witch. He was also convinced that the child was her familiar and not a natural child at all. He now saw the loss of his ship and his being stranded on the beach as a divine intervention to send him on his sacred mission.

With this goal in mind, he set out to uncover positive evidence that Cora was, indeed, a practicing black witch and that she should be punished as such. It was easy enough to construe the strange behavior described by the local people as behavior typical of a witch. Although they would make no formal accusation, the locals talked with relative freedom to Captain Blood, who seemed to talk like a preacher. He made it a point to seek them out and question them.

Of course, all this scurrying about to gather evidence resulted in considerable talk and speculation and even some division of opinion. The Salem captain might have been discouraged to the point of giving up his quest had not a sudden and tragic event occurred just at that time.

Very early one morning some early risers discovered on the ocean beach the dead body of one of the finest young men in the community. There was no apparent cause of death and the young man was lying flat on his back in the wash with an expression of utmost horror on his face. His hands were clasped in an attitude of supplication and on his forehead were burned the digits *666*. Leading away from the body was a single set of footprints of a barefooted person, small and dainty like a woman's footprints. The prints led straight into the nearby woods and there they vanished. It was remembered that there had been a full moon the night before, and the Barbadian crew had kept up quite a racket until after midnight with some sort of voodoo ceremony.

That strange and horrible event set Captain Blood's resolution on fire. Summoning his crew, he questioned them about the preceding night's ceremony and apparently satisfied himself that it was nothing more than an ordinary full-moon orgy which he had seen several times before. With his crew at his heels he went straightway in search of Cora. The islanders followed at what they considered to be a safe distance, fascinated but terrified at what they halfway expected to see.

The witch trial that followed was conducted with all the detail of a typical Salem charade with the stranded captain filling the roles of detective, prosecutor, and judge. They had found Cora in her soundside shack preparing breakfast for herself and the child. Seized and accused of the crimes of witchcraft and murder, she denied the charge and steadfastly and stoutly denied any knowledge of the death of the young fisherman on the beach.

Of course, there were no eye witnesses to testify so, turning to his professional skills as a wizard or white witch, Blood then proceeded to put her to the "test." He ordered his crewmen to bind Cora right wrist to left ankle and left wrist to right ankle and they carried her out into the sound and threw her into the water. There she floated in the shallows, face down. Blood immediately claimed this to be proof positive of her guilt. No matter that the water was shallow and calm. If she had not been a black witch, she would have surely sunk.

Dragging the bedraggled woman ashore, Captain Blood then drew his case knife and tried to cut her hair. Apparently he failed in this because he said later that her hair was tougher than wire rope, an unfailing characteristic of a witch.

One final test remained. Having his crew fill a basin with water from the sound, he required each one of them to prick his finger with a knife and drop several drops of blood into that water. He stirred this liquid until it frothed and then, intoning some chant of his own devising, he stared into the basin. "It is her!" he screamed. Then he passed the container to each of the crew who, in turn, gazed into the bloody liquid and proclaimed in broken English that they saw not only the face of Cora but the face of the Devil peering over her shoulder. Cora only glared at each of them and whispered something in the child's ear.

Without more ado, Cora was untied and then bound securely with heavy rope to the trunk of a nearby live oak tree, the baby in her arms. The ship's crew then gathered a large pile of dry branches from the forest and spread them about the feet of the woman. Flint and steel were then produced and the resulting spark ignited a large pine knot torch which Captain Blood held in his hand. "Confess, Cora, confess before you die!" he roared. The bound woman only snarled at him.

While all this was going on, the island folk were watching in frightened apprehension, too enthralled by what was happening to go away and yet mortally terrified at what they were convinced they were about to see. "Oh, no! Not the baby!" some of the women were heard to murmur, while others could only moan.

Lighted torch in hand, the captain took a step toward the dry wood piled around Cora's feet and was raising the torch when he felt a strong hand on his forearm. Looking up, he saw that the restraining hand belonged to Captain Tom Smith, one of the most respected captains on the island.

"Nay, Captain Blood," said the local. "We cannot permit you to execute this woman. Witch she may be and murderess as well but we have civil courts on the mainland who are more versed in this than we. That is the proper court—"

As he was speaking, Smith was interrupted by one of the other captains.

"My God, Cap'n Tom," the man screamed. "Look, LOOK!"

Turning toward the tree, Captain Smith beheld a sight that would haunt him for the rest of his life. The child in the woman's arms was turning into a huge cat. Hate filled its green eyes and its red mouth opened in a vicious snarl, exposing brilliant white teeth. Not a black cat, mind you, but a tawny feline much like a huge wildcat. With a snarl of defiance, the cat sprang from the woman's arms and sped away into the maritime forest.

Once again Captain Blood strode with his lighted torch toward the tree. Too horrified and awed by what they had seen, the islanders could not stay him this time. Even Captain Smith was staring in wide-eyed, openmouthed amazement, incapable of speech or movement.

Up until that moment the day had been a beautiful one with a clear sky and brilliant sunlight. Suddenly, however, there boiled in from the sound one of the biggest and blackest clouds ever seen in those often stormy parts. The dark blanket of cloud spread over the sky like black ink poured into a pan of white milk. As the onlookers stared in disbelief, a huge clap of thunder sounded and, out of the black cloud bank, there flashed a blinding bolt of lightning.

Striking the live oak near the crown of the tree, the bolt split the already ancient forest giant from top to bottom. There was a strong smell of sulphur and brimstone and the whole group, Barbados crewmen, Captains Blood and Smith, and the islanders fell to their knees, blinded and choking for breath in a cloud of smoke.

When the smoke cleared, there was no sign of Cora. The ropes were still there around the tree and the dry kindling was still piled, untouched, about its base, but of Cora, no sign. No sign, that is, except the split tree and four distinct letters, *CORA*, freshly burned deep into the heart of the tree.

Well, that is the story of the Cora Tree. So far as is known, she was never heard of again in that part of Carolina. But there are those who will tell you in all sincerity that this is not the case with the huge cat. Known only as "The Wampus Cat," it still lives and frequently terrorizes the populace of several coastal counties, or so they say. But that is another story for another time.

The Cora Tree still stands. It is today as much a part of the Outer Banks as the lighthouse at Cape Point or Ocracoke Inlet. The powers that be have had the wisdom to protect this ancient forest giant. It is sincerely hoped that they will continue to preserve this relic of the rich folklore of our region.

Ephraim's Light

IN NORTHAMPTON COUNTY, up near the Virginia border, lies the quiet and pleasant little North Carolina town of Seaboard. Located at the junction of two paved highways, it is quite near historic Halifax. Seaboard itself is also immersed in colonial and antebellum history of the Old North State.

On the outskirts of town there stands a very old and stately relic of pre—Civil War days, a plantation home known as the Woodruff House after the family who owned it in those very early days. This home was the centerpiece of a large and prosperous plantation and at one time several slave houses were located nearby. Nearly two hundred years ago, in the early 1800s, the plantation was a large operation even by the standards of the time. There were many acres of cotton and corn and other grains as well as pasture land for the cattle and hogs, which were an important part of the self-sustaining household.

The house as it now stands is similar to many other Southern plantation manses that have endured to the present day with one exception. With no regularity or predictability, there appears in the downstairs rooms very late at night a weird, yellowish light that flits from room to room, finally ceasing as abruptly as it began and leaving no trace of its having been there. Many people in Seaboard have seen it and many have tried to explain it with different theories. Although some scoff at it, they all agree on its name. To them, it has been for generations "Ephraim's Light." It dates from the antebellum days when Woodruff Plantation was a busy and productive farm.

Most of the labor necessary for such a plantation was furnished by slaves. The owner at that time, a Mr. Martin Woodruff, owned and kept a number of them. He was considered to be a good master, as masters go. He was concerned with the health and well-being of his slaves, had them housed in very comfortable quarters, and provided adequate medical attention for them. He would not break up a family by selling one member and allowed them to earn credits toward the purchase of their own freedom by special or meritorious work. One of his former slaves, thus manumitted, actually lived nearby and owned slaves of his own. Woodruff trained some of the more intelligent slaves to be his house servants, although they would be called back to the fields to save the crops and livestock whenever emergency arose. Most of them seemed to be reasonably content and resigned to their lot, with one exception.

One slave, a large, muscular, black man whom Woodruff had bought "right off the ship" in Boston harbor, turned out to be of a different ilk. He had been a young adult when captured by the Yankee slavers and brought to this country. He resented the whites for his capture and enslavement, although his own tribe habitually captured and kept slaves in his homeland. His name was Ephraim.

Another slave on the plantation was an ancient black man who was so old that he went simply by the name of Adam. The old man was somewhat of an historian and he prided himself on his detailed knowledge of the history of his own tribe as well as the surrounding tribes in the land from which he had been taken. Thus it was that Adam recognized Ephraim as the son of one of the tribal rulers in his homeland. Adam soon made the new slave acquainted with his probable background. Their languages were very similar and they could converse freely. Adam counseled discretion and moderation until an opportunity arose to escape. The young man would have none of that. He studied the crude maps Adam drew in the dirt illustrating the best ways to travel to the Dismal Swamp where so many runaway slaves found sanctuary, but his attitude remained belligerent.

Although he was highly intelligent, he was a malcontent from the start. There was no guile in him and very little discretion. Old Adam served as interpreter for the new slave, but Ephraim soon learned enough English to make himself understood. He was stubborn and resentful and often argumentative with the field bosses and with Woodruff. Things went from bad to worse for Ephraim in spite of Adam's warnings, and Woodruff finally told him that, come November, he was going to take him down to Fayetteville and "put him in his pocket," which was the expression of the day for selling a slave and pocketing the money.

Ephraim was furious. He cursed Woodruff to his face and declared that Woodruff would have a hard time getting him to Fayetteville. All the slaves had heard of the slave market in that city and they were deathly afraid of it. Most of them knew that they had a good situation compared with some other plantations, and they wanted to keep it. There were good masters and there were bad masters, and whether an owner was good or bad made a great deal of difference in the daily lives of these people. The whole concept of slavery was wrong and unjust and unChristian, but most of the slaves had no choice but to make the best of it.

It was only a couple of days after this last confrontation when the slave cursed his owner that a terrific commotion broke out one night in the slave quarters. There were shouts and screams and much running back and forth. When the Woodruff family went out to investigate, they found Mr. Martin Woodruff dead, with several large, gaping wounds about his face and head. Bending over the lifeless figure of his master, the slave Ephraim was lifting the head and shoulders of the dead man. Blood was running down Ephraim's fingers and up his arms. He was absolutely silent and answered not at all when he was asked to explain.

In the confusion that followed, the running back and forth and the desperate efforts to revive Woodruff, Ephraim was left unguarded for a moment, and that moment was all he needed to vanish from the scene. He knew the surrounding countryside very well and he broke and ran to the south, hoping to gain the mighty Roanoke River. If he could get to that waterway, he hoped he could steal a small boat and make his way downstream. Once down in the Albemarle Sound, he thought he could make his way up to the Dismal Swamp where Adam had told him his chances for hiding were excellent. The rivers and sounds were the main arteries of travel in those days, and if he could travel at night and remain hidden during the day, he stood a very good chance of eluding pursuit.

He almost made it. Keeping to the wooded sections and the creeks and streams, he finally came to the low grounds of the Roanoke. It was the fall of the year and it was cold and he had trouble keeping out of the sink-holes and sloughs on his journey. Many times he lost his way and had to retrace his steps, always striving to go downstream, knowing that in that way he must eventually reach the river.

Back at the plantation the alarm had gone out. Repeated rifle shots into the air had brought the neighbors on the run and pursuit was quickly organized. One neighbor owned a pair of bloodhounds which he called "tracking dogs" and these were pressed into service. The youngest and most able-bodied men were selected to form the search party. The dogs were immediately made acquainted with Ephraim's scent and off they all went in full cry. Except for the noise of the dogs, it was a completely silent proceeding save for occasional remarks between the members of the posse. Even the dogs soon fell silent and went about their business of tracking the fugitive with silent, deadly efficiency.

In the cold light of dawn they found him, soaking wet and crouched in a reed thicket on the bank of the Roanoke River. The dogs made no effort to harm their quarry but simply circled him and growled very low in their throats. Their job was done and they knew it. All they wanted then was to go back to their kennels and catch up on their sleep. Not so the men who had caught the slave.

By the time the posse with their captive had returned to Woodruff Plantation, the macabre but loving task of preparing the body for the customary wake was in progress. There was no secure place to keep Ephraim, so he was imprisoned in a smokehouse. A sliding bar placed across the only door prevented its being opened from the inside. A small smoke vent was the only other opening in the stout building.

During all this time the slave had not spoken a word. When asked why he committed the murder, he only stared at his questioners in silence. Even old Adam, who requested to go into the smokehouse alone with the prisoner, could get nothing from him. In vain did Adam plead with the younger man to either confess his guilt or else deny it and tell what he knew of the tragedy. To

Adam's assurances that it would go much easier for him either way, Ephraim's response was the same—a stony silence before the old man who had been his friend. At the end, the captive's temper flared and he cursed Adam for a meddler and told him, in effect, to go to hell.

At nightfall the wake began. Friends and neighbors from the surrounding countryside, both black and white, called, "viewed the body," and remained sitting around for varying lengths of time, some remaining with the body and staying awake the entire night. Sometime after midnight the only watchers remaining awake in the parlor where the wake was being held were the same men, now dog-tired, who had formed the posse.

The silence was broken by a soft knock on the door, and it was opened to admit the old man, Adam. Tears streaked his wrinkled face, for he had come to love Woodruff over the years and to know him as a friend and a scrupulously fair man. To the surprise of the men gathered at the wake, he had come to suggest what he called a sure and certain way to determine, once and for all, whether Ephraim was the murderer. Back in the days of his youth, he told them, he had held a position of some responsibility as the oldest son of the medicine man, who was highly respected in the tribe and whose word was taken as law.

It was the way of the tribe, he said, when there was an unsolved murder, to require each member of the tribe to touch the bare flesh of the victim. If nothing happened, the tested member was deemed to be innocent. If and when the real murderer touched the flesh of the deceased, the wounds of that person would reopen and begin to bleed anew as though they had just been inflicted.

The story goes that the men looked at each other in silence and then, without a word, three of them arose, went out into the night, opened the smokehouse, and dragged Ephraim into the parlor. They had to struggle with the big slave to make him touch the body but, finally, they forced his right hand to touch the hand of Woodruff. The wounds on his neck, they say, gushed blood, staining the fresh shirt that had been placed on the body. Ephraim glared but said not one word. The test, however, was enough to confirm the guilt of the accused as far as the others were concerned. In tears, old Adam stumbled from the room.

Why the young men chose the particular method they used to lynch Ephraim then and there in a nearby field will probably never be known. Possibly some of them had been in the Indian wars in the west and had seen or heard about that method of execution. To a stout post used in butchering farm animals for meat, they tied the prisoner and piled dry pine billets of wood around his feet, beginning with the "fat" lightwood so that it would ignite more easily. When the pyre was ready and the victim secured, he was offered one more chance to speak. He was promised that if he would either confess or deny his guilt, he would not be killed that night but would be taken to the county seat and there given a trial. Ephraim maintained his stony silence, the fire was lit, and he was executed.

Not a very pretty story but one that the residents of the area vouch for as utter truth. The light, of a peculiar yellowish color like the color of burning pine, has been known as Ephraim's light ever since that day. Ask any longtime resident of Seaboard or, for that matter, of nearby Gumberry, and the chances are he will tell you the same story. The light is there. It continues. It is accepted by the residents, some of whom claim that it is the restless ghost of Ephraim who cannot find peace until the full story of that awful night is known.

The Ghostly Hornpipe

ONCE ISOLATED AND ACCESSIBLE only with difficulty, the charming village of Ocracoke is now known to most Carolina vacationers if only as a prime spot for a summer holiday. There time does, indeed, sometimes seem to stand still. Not so familiar is what has been preserved in the Town of Portsmouth, just across Ocracoke Inlet from the village. Now only a memory, Portsmouth was at one time a very important port of entry for oceangoing commerce.

The region was already growing steadily at the beginning of the eighteenth century. Hatteras Inlet to the north was shoaling up, and more and more sea traffic began to use Portsmouth. Ocracoke Inlet, then as now, was very tricky and changeable and a local pilot was needed to bring an incoming vessel past the sand bars and shoals. For this reason there grew up a straggling tent city near the present site of Ocracoke Village which was populated by professional pilots who knew the inlet well. They located here to be on the lookout night and day for incoming merchant ships needing a local pilot. Portsmouth was the destination of these vessels, and the wharves and docks, chandleries and saloons and stores of that city welcomed the weary seamen. "Pilot City," later to become Ocracoke Village, was a temporary lodging for the pilots. Most of them maintained homes in or near Portsmouth.

Fishing was also an important industry, and the nearby Gulf Stream and adjacent waters usually provided abundant catches of very marketable fish. Even the inedible menhaden, still known locally as "fatback," was much in demand in the fall and early summer. Farmers, planting their successive crops of corn, followed the ancient practice of the friendly Indians from whom they first learned about this exclusively American grain. From the beginning, the Indians planted a raw fish in each hill of corn, along with four grains of seed. An Indian legend revolved around this practice, and today we realize that this timeless method provided the corn with excellent fertilizer. Thence came the colonial rhyme that the farmer often repeated as he dropped the four grains in the hill: "One for the raven and one for the crow, one to rot and one to grow."

One of the most successful commercial fishermen of Portsmouth Town was a man named Jesse Hawkins. He was very energetic and resourceful and was usually among the leaders of these farmers of the sea. He was economical almost to the point of stinginess and was an expert at "making do" with equipment long after most seafarers would have replaced it with new.

A typical example was his schooner, the *Taurus*, which he had purchased in Charleston some years before from the widow of a fisherman. Well built, she was admirably suited for the task of offshore fishing but most of her equipment was already old when Hawkins bought her. Her standing rigging was frayed in places and her suit of sails had seen better days. Her anchor cable was an ancient hemp hawser, thick as a man's thigh. It looked strong enough to anchor a continent, but it had held through many a gale and now groaned whenever even a moderate amount of strain was put on the anchor. Her ribs seemed sound, however, and her holds were of ample size to contain large hauls of fish. She was put to use almost the year round as her catches followed the changing seasons. Although he was known as a sometimes reckless skipper, Hawkins had little difficulty in obtaining a competent crew. He was known to be a fair man, if a hard driver, and his crews usually prospered as he prospered.

Competition among the fishing vessels was intense but friendly. Most of the fishing was done on "shares," as the captain and the crew shared the proceeds from whatever catch they made. Although the captain was in full command, the crew had a vested interest in the success or failure of each trip. Often the difference between a highly successful voyage and a commonplace one was the luck or the hustle of getting to the offshore fishing grounds early. The more successful skippers put to sea in the late afternoon and anchored overnight on the edge of the best fishing spots to await the daylight.

Thus it was that on the first night of the full moon in November, 1714, the schooner *Taurus* was anchored just inside the Outer Slough waiting for the first light of day to begin what they hoped should be, by all the signs and portents, a very successful fishing trip. Several hundred yards to the south of the schooner the sloop *Goodfortune* rode easily to her anchor in the increasing swells. Much smaller than the *Taurus* but much newer and more nimble, she was captained by young Arthur Newby, another of the more able fishermen of Portsmouth. He, too, had gone out early to be on hand near the best fishing spots when the expected heavy run of fish began. The crews of each vessel could see the lights of the other as they rose and fell with the motion of the sea.

It is strange, indeed, that neither of the captains noticed the steady falling of the glass, as the barometers were called. Both were accustomed to the frequent, sudden changes in the weather at this time of the year but perhaps they were both preoccupied. Even so, the growing size of the waves which now began to break over the shoals should have alerted them to the fact that something was up weatherwise. Maybe they anticipated only a brief squall which they could handle with ease.

One by one the stars were blotted out by the incoming line of clouds and finally the moon itself grew dimmer and dimmer and finally was completely obscured by the cloud bank. No lights whatsoever were visible in the blackness except for the anchor lights of the two vessels and an occasional wave of phosphorescent fire in the depths of the sea. The wind song slowly changed from a low moan to a higher and higher pitched scream as the full force of the winter storm struck.

All hands were called up on deck on both vessels as the experienced seamen sought to secure all loose gear and ready their craft for the full impact of the blow. It was not long in coming. Line squalls are infamous for the brute force of their initial attack, and this one was unusually fierce even for November in this graveyard of ships. Both captains elected to stay at anchor rather than cut loose and run before the storm. As the seas grew higher and higher, both craft jerked more and more forcibly against their anchors and even experienced sailors were thrown to the deck. Both vessels were securely anchored and both tried to pay out a bit more anchor cable to ease the snatching caused by the waves.

Suddenly, and with an ear-splitting crack, the anchor cable of the *Taurus* parted under the strain and the large schooner was at the mercy of the wind and surf. "Release the jib!" roared Captain Hawkins, and his crew sprang to unfurl this foremost of the sails to gain some control. The jib sail filled and bellied out in the gale all right and was beginning to bring the bow of the ship downwind but in the next instant it split wide open with a sound like that of a cannon firing. The foresail suffered the same fate, as the old canvas could not withstand the full force of the storm. *Taurus* was a derelict out of control and directly upwind now from the anchored *Good-fortune*.

Captain Hawkins could do nothing at this point to control his vessel as she bore down, headlong, upon the smaller *Goodfortune*. Seeing the danger, Captain Newby cast off from his anchor and was beginning to turn his vessel around, but in the instant that she was broadside the *Taurus*, the larger schooner struck her amidships and rolled her over and over under its keel, cutting her almost in two and sinking her with all hands. Hawkins threw overboard all his life preservers and some of his hatch covers in the faint hope that some members of the crew could be saved, but it was to no avail.

Taurus brought up on a sand bar off a lee shore on the southern end of Portsmouth Island. She was easily refloated two days later with no loss of life. Under a jury rig, she limped back into Portsmouth harbor and was later repaired and refitted at the ship's chandlery there. Some of the wreckage of the *Goodfortune* washed up on the southern shore of the island, but no bodies were ever recovered.

As the details of the wreck spread through the port, there was some muttering among the seamen against Captain Hawkins.

"'E shouda reploiced that anchor cable long ago," some said.

"'E's to bloime for the drowndin' of them poor lads and 'e's the one what sent 'em to their deaths unshriven and unburied to roll about the bottom o' the sea 'till kingdom come. 'E ought to be brought to account," others whispered. "Poor dears, they'll never rest."

Most of the townfolk defended the captain. No one could know that the great cable would fail. After all, they argued, he was an experienced captain and surely he would not have placed his own life in danger if he had ever dreamed that such a thing could happen. Time went by. The *Taurus* was refitted with all new cordage and a brand-new suit of sails and the day came when she was ready to put to sea again. Captain Hawkins had visited all the families of the dead crewmen and expressed his sorrow at the tragedy. The families were used to danger and to tragedy on the sea, and they reassured him that they in no way held him to blame.

Well, the schooner was ready and Captain Hawkins was ready, and so plans were made to return to the business of fishing to try to recoup the heavy expense of refitting the vessel. He had not the slightest difficulty in recruiting the same crew of experienced seamen who had sailed with him before. Late one sunny afternoon they put out again through Ocracoke Inlet and out to sea. Once again they anchored near the same spot as before to wait for the first light of day. They all agreed it was an excellent place to begin a day's fishing. In the murky light just before dawn, they set their nets and marked the place with net buoys. The sea seemed to be alive with fish and they anticipated sharing in a near record catch. All day long they left those nets in place and, as the sunny afternoon turned into the early darkness of November, they prepared to haul them in.

Prepared is all they did. As they began to haul in the line attached to the first net, the whole sea and the deck of their ship was suddenly bathed in a mysterious, greenish light. There, in that ghostly light on the deck, they beheld to their horror the spirits of the dead seamen from the little *Goodfortune*! Without a word, the ghosts began to haul in the nets and dump the catch into the hold of the schooner. With precision they performed all the duties that go with bringing such nets aboard and emptying them. All the laboring fishermen had obviously drowned—they had wet hair streaming down to their waists, gaping mouths, and sightless, staring eyes. They made no sound but each ghost went about his task with the sureness and skill of much experience. They worked together to secure the catch like the well-trained team they were. The crew of the *Taurus* could only cower against the masts and the cabin and stare at this apparition with wild and frantic eyes. Many repeatedly crossed themselves and pleaded aloud for divine protection.

As the last bight of the last net was emptied into the hold, there came a brilliant flash of blue-green light and then utter darkness and silence except for the gentle swish of the seas running alongside the ship. The ghosts of the drowned seamen vanished as quickly as they had come. A trembling Captain Hawkins gave the orders to bring his vessel about. In silence he conned her through the inlet and to the dockside in Portsmouth. Once safely docked, he got a lighted lantern and went down into the hold of his ship to estimate his catch. There was not one single fish in the craft! Not one fish of any kind! The hold of the *Taurus* was as empty as when he had set out on this venture. Some of the crew crowded down into the hold behind him and cried out in disbelief and wonder.

The nets were strewn about the deck but none of them was torn or in any way the worse for wear. There were just no fish, but with their own eyes the crew had seen thousands of them dumped into the hold!

Captain Jesse Hawkins was able to obtain crews for just two more fishing trips offshore. The first crew was a full crew, although it contained none of his original personnel. The same thing happened, although they fished an entirely different area of the ocean. The same ghostly group of men fished the nets with exactly the same results—nothing. The second crew was really about half a crew, just enough men to handle the schooner and several of them were drunk by the time they came aboard. No matter. The outcome was exactly the same and they made the trip back to the safety of the dock in record time.

After that, no one would sail with Captain Hawkins again. The *Taurus* stayed tied up to the wharf and gradually rotted away from neglect. She grew less and less seaworthy as shipwrights refused to work on her and prospective buyers would have none of her. Finally, she rotted away and sank at her moorings. No effort was ever made to salvage anything from her or to remove her. She was truly a landlocked derelict.

The haunted captain disappeared from Portsmouth Town and was never seen there again. Some say that he took up piracy as a crewman aboard one of the pirate raiders which began to become more numerous a short time later. Others claimed that he committed suicide and that, at his end, the devil was there to claim him. At any rate, he was never heard from again.

Not so the *Taurus*. There were people who swore that if you went to the spot where she had sunk on any moonlit midnight in the month of November, you could see a strange, ghostly light illuminating her sunken decks. There, by that light, you would see a terrifying sight.

Back and forth upon the sodden and rotted decks, they say, the drowned fishermen of the *Goodfortune* dance a macabre dance, a sailor's hornpipe! Back and forth and round and round they dance in an intricate sort of quadrille which, for centuries, has been the sailor's dance. There is old Pegleg Henry with his accordian playing the tune. The leader of the hornpipe appears to be one-eyed Jack Austin with his black eye-patch. These and all the other departed comrades whom the people of Portsmouth Town had known so well. All the people who knew these departed fishermen are themselves dead now, and Portsmouth Town is but a ghost of its former busy, bustling self. Just a few structures have been preserved for posterity to see and admire.

Some people contend that the ghostly hornpipe continues to this day. They claim that if you can get the operator of a small boat to take you to the spot on any November night with a bright moon, you will be rewarded with a strange sight. Gaze down into the deep water where the *Taurus* finally went to rest and they aver that you will see the ghosts and watch their hornpipe. They say that this will continue until the day of judgment, when the souls of those poor drowned crewmen and their captain will receive the peace and rest they so desperately desire.

Sir William
Shakespeare's Wreck

LIVING IN MODERN-DAY AMERICA, most of us are conscious of our past history—the colonies, the Revolution, the War of 1812, etc. Most of us are also aware of William Shakespeare, the Bard of Avon and possibly England's greatest playwright. Seldom do we think of them in context, yet William Shakespeare was alive and producing plays at the time of our early settlement. He was very much aware of what was going on in colonial America.

It is not known with any certainty whether Shakespeare was financially involved with the Virginia Company, which was formed to colonize this country. It is known that he was a close friend of both the Earl of Southampton and the Earl of Pembroke, both of whom were principals in that company, which was underwriting the Jamestown experiment in what is now Virginia. It was in the early 1600s, and these men and others were mortgaging themselves to the hilt to provide money to keep the fledgling settlement going in the New World.

The little colony was very much in need of more settlers and of supplies so, on June 2, 1609, a fleet of nine ships set sail from Plymouth Harbor in Devonshire bound for Virginia with a total of more than five hundred colonists aboard. In charge of the flotilla was one Sir George Somers, an experienced navigator and seaman. His flagship, the *Sea Venture*, was thought to be the most seaworthy of the fleet. One of its passengers, Sir Thomas Gates, was to be the new governor of the colony. Some reports of the departure indicate that Sir William Shakespeare, the playwright, was present on the docks that day with his noble friends to bid farewell to the little band of ships. At any rate, all was optimism and happiness on that occasion. Relatives and well-wishers of the travelers were on hand to bid them Godspeed, and departure gifts were overflowing, as were smiles and fluttering kerchiefs. The weather was beautiful and it was early enough in the summer for them to feel fairly safe from the gales and storms that sometimes lashed that distant coast later in the year. The *Sea Venture*, as were the other vessels, was well found and manned by competent seamen. All the omens seemed favorable.

The winds and the weather were cooperative and the progress was excellent as the little flotilla made its way westward. On July 24, however, the skies began to darken and the winds increased until one of the most violent hurricanes ever experienced scattered the little fleet, leaving them completely out of touch with each other. The storm struck in the vicinity of what was called the Bermoothes Islands (*sic*) or Ilands (*sic*) of the Devil, and it is a real wonder that any of the ships survived. Mariners of that day considered these islands to be uninhabitable, the dwelling place of evil spirits and ghosts and devils waiting to destroy honest seamen. It was a landmark but also a place to be avoided.

In the weeks that followed the storm the remainder of the ships straggled into Jamestown one by one, with tales of terrible hardship and deprivation. The flagship *Sea Venture* did not appear and was given up for lost in the hurricane. The new governor was presumed to be drowned at sea along with Sir George Somers and all the other passengers and crew of that unlucky ship. *Sea Venture* was indeed lost but not the people on board. The little vessel apparently came up against the very heart of the hurricane, but she was stoutly built and capably handled and she finally came to rest wedged tightly between two pinnacles of rock just offshore from what we now know as Bermuda, but which they verily believed to be the habitat of the devil himself.

More than a year later, the news of the stranding arrived in England. At first it was not made public but came in the form of letters and reports from those responsible for the safety of the colonists. Although this was private correspondence and was not made public until very much later, the Bard of Avon was undoubtedly privileged to read the confidential reports and he knew all the details long before the general public did.

The most detailed of these reports was contained in a letter to the leaders of the Virginia Company by one William Strachey who was on board the *Sea Venture*. The letter was dated July 15, 1610 but, believe it or not, it was not made public until 1625! If you can stand a little of the old English language, here is an excerpt from that letter:

> A dreadful storm and hideous began to blow from out the northeast, which swelling and rearing as it were by fits, some hours with more violence than others, at length did beat all light from heaven; which like a hell of darkness turned black upon us, so much more fuller of horror, as in such cases horror and fear use to overrun the troubled and overmastered senses of all which, (taken up with amazement) the ears lay so sensible to the terrible cries and murmurs of the wind, and distraction of our company, as who was most armed and best prepared was not a little shaken.
>
> For four and twenty hours the storm in a restless tumult had blown so exceedingly, as we could not apprehend in our imagination any possibility of any greater violence, yet did we still find it, not only more terrible, but more constant, fury added to fury, and one storm urging a second more outrageous than the former; whether it so wrought upon our fears or indeed met with new forces. Sometimes shrieks in our ship amongst women and passengers not used

to such burly and discomforts made us look one upon the other with troubled hearts and panting bosoms; our clamors drowned in the winds, and the winds in thunder. Prayers might well be in the heart and lips, but drowned in the outcries of the officers. Nothing heard that could give comfort, nothing seen that might encourage hope. . . . It could not be said to rain, the waters like whole rivers did flood in the air. . . . Here the glut of water (as if throttling the wind erstwhile) was not sooner emptied and qualified but instantly the winds (as having gotten their mouths now free and at liberty) spake more loud and grew more tumultus and malignant. . . . There was not a moment in which the sudden splitting or instant oversetting of the ship was not expected.

Howbeit, this was not all. It pleased God to bring a greater affliction yet upon us; for in the beginning of the storm we had received a mighty leak. And the ship. . .was grown five foot suddenly deep with water above her ballast, and we almost drowned within whilst looking when to perish from above. This, imparting no less terror than danger, ran through the whole ship with much fright and amazement, startled and turned the blood, and took down the braves of the most hardy mariner of them all, insomuch as he that before happily felt not the sorrow of others, now began to sorrow for himself when he saw such a pond of water so suddenly broken in, and which he knew could not. . .but instantly sink him.

Once, so huge a sea brake upon the poop and

quarter upon us, as it covered our ship from stem to stern, like a garment or a vast cloud, it filled her brim full for awhile within, from the hatches up to the spar deck . . . with much clamor encouraged and called upon others; who gave her up now, rent in pieces and absolutely lost!

Did you ever hear a better description of a hurricane right down to the last details—the torrent of rain, the howling winds, and the storm surge, as well as the sense of utter helplessness and abject terror?

The report of colonist Strachey continues:

During all this time the heavens looked so black upon us that it was not possible the elevation of the pole might be observed; not a star by night nor sunbeam by day was to be seen. Only upon the Thursday night, Sir George Somers, being upon the watch, had an apparition of a little round light, like a faint star, trembling, and streaming along with a sparkling blaze, half the height of the mainmast, and shooting sometimes from shroud to shroud, tempting to settle, as it were, upon any of the four shrouds. And for three or four hours together, or rather more, half the night it was with us, riding sometimes along the mainyard to the very end and then returning. At which Sir George Somers called divers about him and showed them the same, who observed it with much wonder and carefulness. But upon a sudden, toward the morning watch, they lost the sight of it and knew not what way it made.

> The superstitious seamen make many con-
> structions of this sea fire, which nevertheless is
> usual in storms; the same . . . which the Gre-
> cians were wont in the Mediterranean to call
> Castor and Polux . . . and . . . the Spaniards call
> it Saint Elmo, and have an authentic and miracu-
> lous legend for it.

Thus, the distressed seamen knew the apparition to be St. Elmo's Fire and each interpreted it in his own way, some as an omen of certain and imminent doom, others as a sign that the patron saint of sailors was about to save them. Each person reacted accordingly. Some of the doomsayers proceeded to go below where, waist-deep in water, they broke open the ship's store of liquor and bade each other long farewells as they drank. The opti- mists, most of them, fell to their knees on deck where they secured a strong handhold against the pitching of the vessel and prayed to St. Elmo.

At that moment, continues Strachey in his report, "Sir George Somers, when no man dreamed of such happi- ness, discovered and cried land. . . . We were forced to run her ashore as near land as we could which brought us within three-quarters of a mile of shore."

Of course, the actual grounding was more luck than skill. They put the helm hard over, all right, to head for the vaguely seen shore. According to the report, the ship heeled over so far and so sluggishly that they thought she would surely capsize and sink under that raging sea. The vessel slowly righted herself, however, and just at that instant a huge grandaddy wave lifted her high toward the heavens and then, just as suddenly, dropped her with a splintering crash tightly between two jutting pinnacles of rock, the tips of submerged mountains such as make up most of the Bermuda atolls. There she was held firm and fast and all the savagery of the storm could not dislodge her.

They were pretty sure they knew where they were. They had been told repeatedly that the Bermoothes were truly islands of the devil to be avoided at all costs. Even Columbus, back from his voyage of discovery to the New World, reported that he had observed a huge ball of fire hanging in the heavens in that vicinity and that he had made haste to put as many sea miles between his ships and the island as he possibly could. So here was a pitiful little band of drenched and terrified seamen and would-be colonists held pinched between two peaks on the shore of the devil's island. The officers knew exactly where they were, but they were as terrified as the rest. It is small comfort to be sure of exactly where you are when you are stuck at the very gates of hell. That is exactly what they believed with all their superstitious hearts. Before you laugh at them, remember that thousands of people this very day are deathly afraid of what they call the "Bermuda Triangle"!

A couple of days passed and then the need for fresh drinking water became acute. The ship's stores had been spoiled by the sea water, and what water was on hand in the ship's kegs was unfit to drink. The weather had turned beautiful, as it usually does after a hurricane, and the land ashore yonder did not look too forbidding in the daylight. They finally decided to let a few of the bravest souls take the longboat, which somehow had been lashed down tightly enough to escape major damage in the storm, and explore the island in search of food and especially water. The rest of the survivors watched in trepidation as the little craft pulled away from the entrapped *Sea Venture* under the power of four sets of oars.

When the longboat returned to the wreck that afternoon, they brought amazing and heartening news. They had found fruits and berries in abundance and other edible plants of many kinds, as well as pools of fresh water caught in the rocks from the recent storm. Thus reassured, the whole ship's company abandoned the wreck of the *Sea Venture* and traveled by the longboat to the shore. There they set up crude habitations from the branches of trees and shrubs, which were later replaced by huts built from timbers washed up from the wreck of their ship. Instead of a living hell complete with devils, they had found a verdant paradise full of food for the taking.

To continue the excerpt from the report of William Strachey to the Virginia Company:

> Sure it is that there are no rivers nor running springs of fresh water to be found on any of them (islands). When we came first, we digged and found certain gushings and bubblings which, being either in bottoms or on the sides of hanging grounds, were only fed with rain water which nevertheless soon sinketh into the earth and vanisheth away, or emptieth itself out of sight into the sea without any channel above or on the surface of the earth. For, according as

their rains fell, we had wells and pits (which we
had digged) either half full or absolute exhausted and dry, howbeit, some low bottoms
we found to continue as ponds or standing
pools, continually summer and winter full of
fresh water.

There were also birds on the island, some so tame that
they could be captured by hand, and the waters around
the shore were full of good fish and clams and oysters.
The climate was very mild both in summer and winter,
and they might have lived on there in comfort the rest of
their days but soon talk began of trying to reach Jamestown in some way. They had no hope whatsoever that
anyone would come looking for them in a place which
theretofore had had such a bad reputation and which
was avoided by all mariners. There was actually a mutiny
of sorts when several men wanted to seize the longboat
and try to make it to the Virginia settlement. The plan
was discovered, however, and was suppressed by Sir
George Somers. Yet so persistent was the longing for relatives and friends and homes that the same plan was
brought up again and a compromise was reached.

Several of the most trusted and able men, with the
first mate in charge as skipper, were to take the longboat
and try to make it over the open sea to Jamestown to
bring help. Being expert navigators, they knew exactly
where Bermuda was located and they knew the exact
course and approximate distance to Jamestown. It was a
relatively short distance to the mainland, and these were
men who had lived most of their lives on the sea. The
boat was small, though, and the sea was large and unpre-

dictable. They knew very well the danger, but they decided to take the risks.

Thus the longboat was fitted with a fragment of the torn sails from the *Sea Venture* and laden with casks of fresh water and large baskets of fruit and vegetables and with several plump, roasted fowl, which they had discovered in large flocks on the island. *Sea Venture's* navigational instruments, the sextant, the quadrant, the chronometer, and the charts, were retrieved from the captain's cabin on the wreck and placed aboard the longboat. They loaded oars for eight men in case the wind died on them. Thus prepared and with high hopes, they set out. They were never seen nor heard from again! At least, not in their natural forms.

The days turned into weeks and the weeks into months as the little band on Bermuda became more anxious and discouraged about ever seeing their families again. True, there were no Indians nor anybody else to threaten them here as there were in Virginia. Food was abundant and the sea teemed with fish. The warm waters of the Gulf Stream bathed the shore of the island and the climate was mild the year round. It was actually difficult to tell summer from winter. In spite of all this, they wanted to go home. Home to them now was the little English settlement of Jamestown.

News of the disappearance of the *Sea Venture* had long since reached both Jamestown and England. That portion of the expedition had been given up as lost at sea in the hurricane. No one was looking for them and no one in his right mind would have dared to venture close to the Isle of the Devil, even if he had been searching for them. So far as the civilized world knew, it was a closed book—another unexplained disappearance at sea, an event not at all uncommon in that period of history.

To the marooned Englishmen and women the book was not closed. Born to the sea and nurtured in a climate of freedom, they just never gave up. When it finally became obvious to even the most hopeful that the longboat was not going to return and that no one was ever going to search for them, they began to plan to rescue themselves. They determined to see if they could build a boat seaworthy enough to carry them to the nearby Carolina coast which, at that time, was still a part of the colony of Virginia. The only tools they had were the tools of the ship's carpenter, which had been salvaged from the wreck. The only materials were what little standing timber was available and, of course, the *Sea Venture* herself.

Binding several logs together with strong vines, they began to go back and forth from the stranded vessel to the beach, gradually dismantling the ship board by board and timber by timber. The larger timbers they floated ashore. The nails in the craft were carefully pulled and then straightened for reuse and were hoarded like so much gold. The ropes and cordage on the *Sea Venture* were much the worse for wear, but some of them were serviceable and they were brought ashore and put in a dry place in one of the huts. The sails were nearly a total loss but some were in pieces large enough to save.

For months the shipbuilding went on, overcoming difficulty after difficulty with the determination that only their bulldog English characters could maintain. It was calculated that one vessel of the size they could launch could not accommodate all the potential passengers, so two craft were built. No one was going to remain behind this time. They were all "going for broke," to either find their new homes and their families or die in the attempt. Considering the odds against them, it was remarkable that their spirits were so high. The air rang with sea chanteys and English songs that they had sung since childhood as the two hammers, one saw, and four chisels were in constant use. While all this was going on, careful calculations were made each day as to just where on the horizon the sun rose and set and where the known constellations rose and set and exactly where Polaris, the constant North Star, was located in the sky. This knowledge might mean the difference between life and death once they were at sea and out of sight of land.

After months of hard and innovative labor, the craft were finished. They certainly did not look like boats but every man and woman hoped and prayed that they would serve as boats. They resembled crude huts built on rafts with poles sticking up in the middle and attached to one pole by vines was a crude yardarm. It took the combined strength of all the people to push each craft down a gentle slope into the calm waters of the huge harbor. There they floated, looking about as makeshift as could be imagined. In a later day, Huckleberry Finn would probably have turned up his nose at them. But they floated. They floated on an even keel and they even had a little freeboard separating the gunwale or rail from the surface of the calm water. Although the shipwrecked crew did not know it, the Polynesians had sailed similar open rafts across great distances in the Pacific Ocean in their migrations from island to island. Of course, many of those Polynesians had also drowned when typhoons had struck. The shipwrecked people of the *Sea Venture* waded, one by one, out to their strange craft and filled his or her allotted space thereon with the most valuable of their possessions. It was the most improbable flotilla and crew imaginable but they were determined, set, and ready to go, come fair weather, hurricane, or shipwreck.

It was a beautiful May morning when the armada set sail. There was not a cloud in the sky, the wind was a gentle easterly breeze, and the sea was almost as calm as a lake as the little creations, sailing in tandem or line astern, headed out to the westward. The younger members of the crew had spent many hours fishing just offshore in a much smaller raft made from shorter logs and they had become familiar with the intricate pattern of reefs and channels around the island. Had they not gained this knowledge, it would have made passage out to the open sea much more difficult.

As soon as those barriers were cleared, the leading boat broke out an English flag and ran it up on the stubby mast to the cheers of the entire group. They were on their way and no turning back was possible now, even if they had wanted to. It was do or die. Although the mainland coast was supposed to be a relatively short distance away, there was much apprehension, and many prayers were offered both silently and aloud for the safe completion of the voyage.

The captain tried to set his course as near to due west as he could, relying on his calculations made during the preceding months. Remember, his compass and all his other navigational instruments as well as his charts were gone, as was his first mate. He knew, even without his charts, that Jamestown lay somewhat north of west, but he also knew the tendency of the current (which men later were to call the Gulf Stream) to veer vessels to the northward. He was trying to allow for the "set" of that current in traveling due west. He counted on the current to push his flotilla to the northward of the course he set.

On they sailed under smiling skies and with a gentle southwest wind following until they made landfall somewhere to the north of Cape Hatteras but well south of Jamestown. This landfall was extremely fortunate for even a small storm could have overwhelmed both his little craft, and no one would ever have known what happened to them. They had once already been given up as lost at sea by friends on both sides of the Atlantic Ocean. Relying on his sailor's sixth sense of direction, the captain decided that he had probably overestimated the strength of the current and so he turned to the northward and sailed up the coast looking for Jamestown and comparative safety.

It so happened that, on the twenty-third day of May, 1610, lacking just exactly ten days from being a full year since their departure from Plymouth, their tiny fleet arrived at Jamestown. When the settlers in that town descried the two strange-looking craft coming to anchor near the town they could not believe their eyes. No such craft had ever been seen, there or elsewhere, and they just could not believe that those rafts had come from the open sea.

The joyful reunions of the families and friends can be imagined. Here was a whole crowd of people, brothers and sisters and cousins and uncles and other loved ones who had been given up for drowned, suddenly reunited! It is said that even the Indians, who had not been known theretofore for their friendliness, took part in the extended celebrations and services of thanksgiving for this miracle. It was, indeed, a miracle.

Word of this wonderful arrival soon spread to England, but only the news that the castaways had been found. No word of the details of the events or how they came about was made public in England. Officials of the Virginia Company received the reports of William Strachey, from which the excerpts above were taken, but these were private communications. They were kept in the private files of the company and, for some reason, were not made public until 1625. But even though these communications were the property of the Virginia Company, it is known that William Shakespeare had access to them and read them avidly.

This was, indeed, grist for his mill. Here was a plot ready-made for one of his most famous plays, taken from real life. Shakespeare's public was very much interested in the Virginia Colony and in the fate of the colonists, but they had only the barest information about this latest effort to reinforce the colony. The audience was ripe, the timing was ripe, and the story needed only the genius of William Shakespeare to be formed into what was, in that day, a smash hit.

Thus the Bard of Avon penned one of his last and one of his greatest plays, *The Tempest*. His characters speak many of the lines that originated in those confidential reports. The play was an instant "hit" and is still regarded to this good day as a major jewel in the crown of the acknowledged king of playwrights. *The Tempest* achieved even more popularity later when the full facts of the real-life adventures of the *Sea Venture* became known to the people of England and Europe.

So ends one of the most traumatic episodes in the colonization of this country. The remarkable thing is that every one of the voyagers who set out from Plymouth was saved and delivered to Jamestown. Everyone, that is, except the brave men who set out in the longboat to bring help. What of them?

Well, there has never been any official explanation of their fate. They simply vanished. There are many people alive today (and most of them very intelligent people) who will tell you that this is just another example of the doom that lurks in the "Bermuda Triangle," that imaginary triangle with its peak at Bermuda and its base along the Atlantic seaboard from Key West to Norfolk. They point to the many ships and even airplanes that have mysteriously disappeared in that area, including the American warship *Wasp* in 1814, the German freighter *Anita*, which left Newport News on March 21, 1973 and was never heard of again, the nuclear submarine

Scorpion, and many, many other vessels that just vanished.

Who knows?

At any rate, it is said that when a hurricane approaches the North Carolina Outer Banks, the oceanside residents of the area around Corolla and Caffey's Inlet have spied a small sailing boat of the general dimensions of a ship's longboat. Sailing briskly to the northward with her tattered sail driving her through the spume-topped waves, she appears to be in serious trouble. Over the rising wind it is said that you can hear from time to time the helmsman of that craft shout in a loud voice and in urgent tones, "Hoy! Be ye the men of Jamestown?" Without waiting for an answer, the helmsman and the little boat speed on to the north and are lost from view.

Who knows?

Doctor Dillard's Treasure

DOCTOR RICHARD DILLARD WAS ONE OF the finest citizens of Edenton and Chowan County. He was a widely known and greatly loved physician who did much good throughout the entire northeastern section of North Carolina. Living on his palatial estate called Beverly Hall near Edenton, he was intensely interested in the history and rich folklore of that region and, ironically, became part of an adventure that would make the area even richer in lore.

In his later years the doctor loved to tell of how he almost became famous as the finder of a fabulous treasure. According to the good doctor, this is the way it happened.

In February 1897, Edenton was a very busy port of

entry to the United States. Much foreign and local water traffic used the port, and the waterfront usually buzzed with the sound of several different languages as the crews enjoyed liberty ashore. Dr. Dillard at that time held the position of surgeon of the port of Edenton. This meant that it was his responsibility to quarantine ships on which there was a contagious disease, to attend to the sick on such vessels, and to patch up the wounds of the visiting seamen, among other things. These duties were in addition to his private practice, so he was usually a very busy man. In February of 1897, tensions were high, for it was just before the outbreak of the Spanish-American war. There was much animosity between American seamen and the Spanish crews who used the port, but it was, of course, the doctor's duty to treat them all.

Early one morning during this uneasy time Dr. Dillard answered a pounding on his door to confront a very swarthy, Spanish-looking seaman who spoke broken English. This stranger finally got it across to the doctor that there was a very sick man on board the ship from which he came and that he wanted the port surgeon to come and look at him. The physician picked up his little black bag, checked it, and went immediately with his visitor to the craft in question.

Even before he boarded the vessel he noticed several strange things about her. The rigging was not familiar to him and the very shape of the hull seemed unusual. Once aboard, he noticed that all the hatches were open and that all the holds of the ship were empty except one, which contained a large, sealed, iron chest.

Going into the cabin he found an extremely sick man lying on a bunk. Dr. Dillard diagnosed the very contagious disease. He immediately ordered the yellow quarantine flag raised so that no one would visit the ship and ordered the two men aboard not to come ashore until he gave permission. The sick man was apparently better educated than the messenger and spoke better English. He gave his name and rank as John Rogers, the captain of the ship. He promised full cooperation with the doctor and the port authorities. He assured the doctor that the two men on the boat were the only crewmen and comprised the entire ship's company. This also surprised the physician, because a vessel that size would normally carry a crew of at least seven or eight men.

Dr. Dillard treated the man daily after that, rowing out in his own skiff and bringing the necessary medicine, until he satisfied himself that his patient was out of danger and would probably not need his services much longer. The port authorities had respected the quarantine and had waited for either the death or the recovery of the sick man before going aboard to fill out the necessary papers for the ship's entry into this country.

Finally, one morning Dr. Dillard went down to the waterfront to lift the quarantine on his way to the boat. As he approached the docks he was astounded to see that the vessel had left the harbor. The port authorities knew nothing about the departure other than the fact that she had slipped her moorings in the night and gone down the sound with a strong west wind. It was all very mysterious. The doctor was sure that all danger of contagion was past, so he dismissed the matter from his mind.

Several days later Dr. Dillard picked up a copy of the *New York Herald* and read a dispatch from a Havana newspaper, which reported that two prominent Spanish officials stationed at Cuba had seized a large amount of Spanish gold coins, conveyed it secretly to their vessel in the harbor, and escaped. The dispatch also stated that a Spanish cruiser was in hot pursuit. All this at a time when the Spanish and American governments were on the brink of war. It would be just a few weeks until the *U.S.S. Maine* would be blown up without warning in the Havana harbor with a loss of two hundred sixty-six American lives.

Dr. Dillard immediately saw the possible connection between his mysterious ex-patient and the news dispatch. The fact that there had been only two people aboard the craft, the fact that all the holds below deck had been empty except for that one sealed, iron chest, and the vessel's abrupt and mysterious departure all added up to one thing. The physician knew in his heart that the strange craft was the fugitive from Cuba laden with gold coins. For days he searched the newspapers for foreign dispatches that might tell him whether or not the Spanish gunboat had captured the fleeing vessel, but to no avail. The shooting war broke out soon after that and all news from Cuba and Spain became heavily censored.

About two years later, after the end of the war, Dr. Dillard found in his mail a letter bearing a Spanish postage stamp. The contents would change the rest of his life. It read as follows:

Citadel of the Alcazar
Toledo, Spain
April 20, 1900

Dear Sir:

You will remember me as the fever patient on the ship in Edenton Bay about two years ago. My real name is Juan Roderigo and not John Rogers as I gave it to you. I was connected with the Insular Treasury at Havana and, realizing the early and inevitable downfall of Spanish power in Cuba, I seized the Spanish funds in my hands amounting to over two million pesos and, with my secretary, chartered a vessel and made safe our escape. Taking suddenly ill at sea, we put in at Hatteras and made our way up to Edenton where I was the recipient of your kindness. I was determined that the gold should never fall into the hands of the Spaniards again. Realizing that we were hunted, we jettisoned the large chest containing the gold at a certain place near the shore of Albemarle Sound below Edenton with my compass carefully taking the bearings and then made a plot or map of the exact spot. We then sailed for the Bermudas to place our-selves under the protection of the English, in-tending, when peace was declared, to return to Edenton and secure our treasure again. But we were unfortunately captured at sea and taken to Spain in irons, my companion (the messenger) dying on the voyage and I am now the sole liv-ing repository of this secret. I was sent at once to the prison of the Alcazar where I am still kept under the strictest espionage. From the very nature of the crime, there will be but little chance for royal clemency toward me for many years to come, for public sentiment is very intent toward me now because Spain is overwhelmed with a sea of debts and needs every possible peso so I make you this offer. If you can find some way to convey to me 200 pesos in some secret manner, that I may have some comforts other than this horrible prison fare, I will give you this map locating the treasure which I have now sewed in the lining of my hat. I have gotten a priest, who visits me every Wednesday, to smuggle this letter out to you. His name is Friar Talivera and you might operate through him.

Adios Señor,
Juan Roderigo
alias John Rogers

Excited beyond belief, the young doctor felt that here was the chance of a lifetime to become rich. All the facts seemed to fit perfectly, so he decided to travel to Spain to seek his fortune. Closing out his affairs as quickly as he could, the doctor traveled to Washington where he obtained his passport to travel through Spain "on pleasure and recreation." He then left for New York, where he booked passage to Spain.

Upon arrival, he traveled overland for some distance, finally arriving at Toledo where he took lodging at a little inn called Fonda del Maria. Realizing that a great deal of red tape and ceremony would have to be endured before he could hope to gain entry into the prison, he

enlisted the help of the newly appointed American consul to Spain, who was spending the summer at Toledo.
He did not take the consul into his confidence but,
rather, told him that he was a kinsman of the prisoner
and wished to visit his cousin to bring him some money,
which he understood could be used to buy small comforts and extra food in prison.

Thus he was able to gain admission to the infamous
Alcazar but was denied a private audience with his
friend and former patient. The prison guard stayed with
him during the few minutes the doctor was allowed in
the cell. Continuing his pretense of bringing relief to a
kinsman, Dillard embraced him, called him cousin, and
counted out $200 in American gold coin. Giving the
gold to the prisoner, the physician wished him well and
turned to depart, whereupon the prison guard took him
by the arm. As Roderigo said his farewells he pointed to
his hat, which lay beside the doctor's hat on a table.
Catching the signal, the alert visitor picked up the prisoner's hat and put it on his head, leaving his own hat
in the cell. It was a little small but he tilted it forward
on his brow at a jaunty angle and walked out of the Alcazar.

Hurrying back to his room at the inn, Dr. Dillard
locked the door, took off the hat, and tore into the lining. There, sure enough, was a large map with courses
and distances marked plainly. Taping the map to his
body, the doctor paid his bill, made his goodbyes, and
immediately left by coach to return to his port of entry.
There he took the very first ship back to New York, the
chart still taped safely to his middle. Back home in Eden-

ton, he took his precious map to his office that night and spread it out on his desk to carefully study it. It was his first real chance to examine it closely as he had been preoccupied with keeping it hidden on the trip home.

It was a beautifully drawn piece of cartography with neat lines indicating courses and distances. But when he examined the top of the map, Dr. Dillard discovered to his dismay that all the instructions and explanations so necessary to interpreting the chart were written in Spanish, a language of which he knew nothing! The location of the treasure was as unknown to him as it had been before.

There is a sort of frenzy that is likely to overtake any treasure hunter, especially when he thinks he is closing in on his prize. There tends to be a more or less continual looking over the shoulder and a haunting suspicion and fear that some stranger knows about it and is plotting to snatch it from him. It happens to the best of us and is a sure sign of treasure-itis. These fears are not groundless, either. There have been a number of cases in which this is exactly what has happened when someone got careless or too trusting of strangers.

In Dr. Dillard's case, what was obviously needed was an English translation. But by whom? Being well aware of the need for secrecy, the doctor could well envision some stranger (or some friend, for that matter) deliberately misinterpreting the map and keeping the secret of the treasure's location for his own later use. The doctor knew no one who spoke Spanish and, even if he had, he did not know whether he could trust anyone with a secret this large. No, he decided, he must keep his secret to himself and discover the treasure by learning the Spanish language. Being highly intelligent and a quick learner, he did not doubt his ability to learn another language rather quickly.

Having already invested so much time and money in this venture, he concluded that the only sure way to keep his secret was to leave the country just long enough to pick up enough Spanish to meet his need. He then journeyed to Cuba, where he was fortunate enough to meet up with a family who took him in as a lodger and bargained to teach him Spanish as well. Concentrating his good brain entirely on this quest, he learned quickly and was soon conversing in Spanish with the local people in Havana. Believing that he was fluent enough in the spoken and written language with a sound working knowledge of the local idiom, he bade goodbye to his Cuban friends, settled up his bills, and took ship back to the United States.

Back in his office in Edenton with his treasure map spread out before him, Dr. Dillard was tickled pink to discover that he could now read the map as readily as though it had been written in English. He had had to take no one into his confidence and his secret was preserved.

According to the doctor's translation, the legend on the map read, in part: "S. 45 degrees E., from a cluster of three cypresses to the sound shore, then along the shore due East exactly 500 yards, then South 68 degrees West, 750 yards. The chest lies at the intersection of these two lines, upon a sandy bottom in 16 feet of water; the three cypresses, the starting point, can easily be found by measuring 1,025 yards due East from ———. Here, of course, is the secret."

The omission represented by the blank line above is the omission of Dr. Dillard himself, but even then it was obvious that the intersection alluded to was out in the sound some distance from the shore.

The doctor found the dry landmarks with comparative ease. He then purchased this land, some twenty-five acres, including the waterfront. This purchase cost him some $1,250, but now he felt that he was hot on the trail of the treasure and he intended to go forward. He believed that owning the land would give him the offshore rights to any object found on the bottom of the sound opposite his property. Hiring a surveyor, the doctor had him run off the lines as he quoted them without showing him the map or revealing why he wanted the lines surveyed except for saying that he was locating a fishing site.

Then another difficulty arose. The map had been so crumpled by frequent handling and by being strapped to the doctor's chest that the readings of the third course were blurred, making it uncertain whether it was "S. 68 degrees W." or "S. 48 degrees W.," which made a great difference. To be absolutely sure, he then had the surveyor run both lines and identify two points of intersection, both out in the sound. Thus he had two possible locations of the treasure. He marked them both by stakes made of green saplings driven into the bottom of the sound in the manner of fish-net stakes. It was now time to try to recover the chest of gold.

Going to Norfolk, he found a wrecking company and,

still without revealing his purpose, chartered a large barge, the type equipped with a windlass used for lifting wreckage from the bottom of fairly deep water. The doctor anticipated that the treasure chest would be extremely heavy and he would need the powerful windlass to raise it. The barge had been moored in the harbor of Charleston, South Carolina.

When it came time to close the deal, however, it was found that the barge was too large and drew too much water to pass through the canal, and the insurance companies refused to insure it for the trip around Hatteras from Charleston. To get things moving again, the doctor, in lieu of marine insurance, entered into a personal bond with the barge owners in the amount of $2,500 to be paid to the owners if the barge was lost. Well, the upshot of that matter was that the tug and the barge it was towing ran into a northeast storm, the towing hawser parted, and the tug lost its tow, which was wrecked off Hatteras for a total loss. That meant that the good doctor had to pay the $2,500 to the owners to honor his undertaking. After that, the winter closed in and the discouraged doctor suspended all further efforts to recover the treasure until the next spring.

When the weather cleared the following spring, Dr. Dillard took a slightly different tack. He hired a professional diver to go down at both the points he had targeted as "intersections" and search for anything unusual. Again in an effort at secrecy, the doctor agreed to operate the air pump from the diver's boat himself. The location of the first intersection proved unfruitful, but the second location was different. The diver had been down but a short while with the doctor manning the air pump when Dr. Dillard was electrified by a series of signals on the hoisting line that the underwater explorer had, indeed, found something that should be brought up. In his excitement and haste to bring the man up and find out what was below, the good doctor accidentally knocked overboard the air hose, which was supplying the diver's breathing air. In his efforts to recover that hose, Dillard lost the line which was used to bring the man to the surface. The poor fellow suffocated before he could be brought up. When he was finally brought to the surface, he was quite dead, and all efforts to revive him failed.

The family of the deceased diver went to court and sued Dr. Dillard for the death of their son. The jury ruled that the equipment was unsafe and that its operation was improper and awarded them some $4,000. The doctor borrowed the money to pay off the judgment and went even more deeply into debt to get money to recompense the dead diver's family, with whom he sympathized.

Now thoroughly discouraged, the physician broke off all efforts to locate the treasure and attempted to "tote up" his losses so far in the effort to achieve a fortune. His balance sheet looked like this:

Amount of Expenses to Toledo, Spain	$ 500.00
Amount paid for Roderigo's map	200.00
Lessons in Spanish	190.00
Three months' board & room in Havana, Cuba	75.00
Expenses at Norfolk	50.00
Paid wrecking co. for loss of barge	2,500.00

Damages for drowned diver	4,000.00
Misc. Expenses and labor	1,000.00
Total	$8,515.00

As assets:

25 acres of land and waterfront	$ 1,250.00
Map locating treasure worth more than	5,000,000.00
	$5,001,250.00

The treasure hunter was understandably depressed. He had spent a young fortune pursuing his dream of wealth, and all he had was a map and twenty-five acres of waterfront property. He could not help but wonder if he had been duped and if the whole thing was a clever plot to bilk him out of his money. He could not forget, however, how all the facts fit together. The Spaniard had really been very sick, the ship had contained no cargo except the iron chest, and the map had been drawn in exquisite detail. In his heart he felt sure that his former patient had not deceived him. At the same time he could not escape the fear that he was pouring money down a rat hole and that, to succeed, he must have financial help.

Dr. Dillard determined in his own mind that the only practical way to discover, once and for all, if the treasure was really there under the waters of the Albemarle Sound was to hire a steam shovel and dredge the entire area. At the prices of that day, he figured that he could charter a steam shovel for about $100 a day, including all necessary expenses. He calculated that it would take about twenty days to complete the work if the weather held good and the water was not rough. That amounted to an additional expense of about $2,000.

At long last the doctor made up his mind that what he must have was someone else to share his dream of wealth and to share the expense of seeking it. On January 27, 1907, he ran a notice in the Charlotte, North Carolina *Observer*, which read in part as follows: "To anyone who will pay one-half of my past expenses and help me charter this dredge, I will give a moiety in the proceeds of this treasure. This would require an advance in cash of $5,257.50. Under no consideration will I allow anyone to examine my map or become half owner in my prospective fortune, or the pursuit of it, until the entire amount is in my hands. . . . All communications should be addressed to: Dr. Richard Dillard, Beverly Hall, Edenton, N.C."

History does not record whether Dr. Dillard received a reply to his newspaper ad. It is not thought that he recovered his treasure, because there was no sudden improvement in his style of living and no disruption of the calm Albemarle Sound waters by a steam shovel, at least not on any large scale. He told this story, always withholding the secrets of the treasure map, as long as he lived. After his death, no trace was ever found of his treasure map, but then remember that he was an expert at concealing it.

The much loved doctor was fond of the legends and stories of eastern North Carolina and even jotted some of them down on occasion. It is known that he traveled to Spain at least once. Was this whole thing a figment of his imagination or was there really a treasure map? He would never say. It may well be that, sixteen feet under the calm waters of Edenton Bay, there rests a fortune in gold coins just waiting for the proper person to come along and claim it. The North Carolina laws concerning the rights of individuals to finds on the sound bottom and even in the oyster gardens have changed. During the last few years alone these laws have been narrowed and so severely defined as to make the chance of finding (and keeping) such a treasure much more difficult even than the hardships that faced the good doctor.

Even so, the fascination and the lure of buried or sunken treasure remains strong in the human breast. Gold, there for the taking?

Scuba diving, anyone?

East Lake Accommodation

TO REALLY UNDERSTAND AND APPRECIATE the true Outer Bankers of North Carolina, one must live with them and be a part of them—not with retirees nor with summer vacationers nor with developers. This is a process that takes not weeks nor months but years and years preferably dating back to the time when life and making a living meant a constant battle with mother sea and with the elements and danger and frequently with hardship.

Such a Spartan and self-reliant life has bred into these hearty people many outstanding characteristics not often found elsewhere. They could and often did resort to innovative and somewhat dangerous ways of keeping food on the table, warmth in the house, and clothes on the backs of their loved ones. These characteristics are present today in the younger generations of coastal people. They do not wear their courage nor their honesty nor their deep religious feeling on their sleeves like a badge, but they are there just the same.

Times were tough on the Banks in the teens. After World War I was over and the German U-boat menace was removed from our coast, the youngsters from the Banks who had served so well in the armed forces returned home to try to rebuild their lives. It was tough going. There were times when the sounds froze over and fishing them or crabbing them or oystering them was impossible. There were weeks on end when the sea just refused to give up the fish and other seafood that many of them depended upon. There were times when some of the best and hardest working families felt the pinch of hunger. They shared what they had with each other but frequently there was just not enough to go around.

Some of our coastal dwellers found meager sustenance by going into the salt marshes in hip boots and harvesting the yaupon which grows so lushly here. This was baled and then shipped north to Baltimore and New York, where people had learned to make and relish yaupon tea. The returns from this enterprise were lean and it is said that some of our people were even reduced to eating seagull eggs when the hens refused to lay. The Outer Bankers understandably do not like to be joked with or looked down upon about these hard times. To this day there are places where you can get into immediate, physical trouble by referring to some of them as "yaupon eaters." They are proud and sensitive people and these sore spots had best be left alone.

This was the situation when, on January 29, 1919, the Eighteenth Amendment to the Constitution of the United States was ratified. This amendment and supporting laws strictly prohibited the manufacture, sale, and/or transportation of intoxicating liquors in or into the United States. The Bankers had never, as a class, been addicted to the use of strong drink. There were exceptions, of course, but by and large they were teetotalers. Indeed, it has been only very recently that even the sale of beer and wine on Hatteras Island is permitted.

Now, the locals were not affected by this sudden drying up of all intoxicating beverages, but not so the rich men who had built posh hunting clubs up and down the coast where they lived in luxury during the hunting seasons and from which they sallied forth, guided by the local residents, to hunt the abundant wildlife. Many of these wealthy sportsmen had longstanding habits of imbibing daily from the flowing bowl and they deeply resented it when their legal sources of supply were cut off. They appealed to their hosts for help in their dilemma and, characteristically, some of the locals tried to help.

One thing that was available and abundant was corn. The windmills to grind the corn were there. The Outer Banks were isolated and barely accessible except by boat and even then help was needed from the local fishermen. A few of those fishermen had learned to set up distilleries of a crude kind and to ferment and then distill the corn mash into a very potent corn liquor. These few taught the art to their kin and interested neighbors and, before long, the visiting sportsmen had a reliable supply of a very strong and very pure intoxicant. Aged in a charred keg and served cold, it was preferred by some of the visitors to the whiskey they had formerly gotten from Canada.

At its inception this was not a business enterprise entered into for profit. The distillers, bootleggers if you will, made but a scant profit over their actual expenses. This was friend dealing with friend and the arrangement went very smoothly for awhile. Some of the imbibers began to give generous tips around Christmas and other holidays but it was more of an accommodation than anything else. Everyone was discreet and the distillers were vigilant in their efforts to make sure that the product was pure and of the very finest ingredients. The universal package was the fruit jar or canning jar.

Inevitably, as the hunters returned to their mainland homes, the fame of the whiskey grew and there began to be demands in the off-season for some of the product to be furnished the sportsmen at their homes. By appointment, boats were sent down to obtain jars of the liquid and soon the manufacture of "moonshine" or "white lightning" became almost a cottage industry. Then pressure began to be applied by the preachers and by some of the church people of the Outer Banks. The whole thing was illegal, they said, and this activity was being carried on sometimes within sight of their homes where the children could certainly see and be impressed. Although there were only a few of these "suppliers," the community as a whole began to express their disapproval.

There was no clear-cut ultimatum but the choice was clear. Either these men who had sought to simply help their friends and employers must quit and run the risk of losing some of the very few profitable jobs in the area or else a new location must be found. Some of them did quit and a few of those did, indeed, lose their jobs with the hunt clubs. A few decided to cast about for a new location that would be far enough away from their homes to satisfy their families and yet close enough to be easily accessible by their boats. The ideal site also had to be sufficiently isolated to minimize the chance of interference by federal agents who were becoming more and more active in areas to the north.

The spot they finally chose seemed almost ideal for those various purposes. Where the Alligator River flows into Albemarle Sound there was (and still is) a largely isolated and uninhabited area of marsh and pocosin land interlaced with canals and waterways and overhung by giant moss-festooned cypress trees. The only residents of the entire area lived a good distance away, along the edges of the marsh. This wild land includes Durant's Island and the marsh north and east of the village of East Lake and west and south of the fishing hamlet of Mashoes. Probably because the only road in the area ran through East Lake, the whole region was known as East Lake. To this day you had better know what you are doing or you will get irretrievably lost in the huge lake or in the smaller South Lake or in Northeast Prong or Deep Bay or in any of the honeycomb of natural canals and guts and sloughs that comprise the area. If there ever was a genuine wilderness, this was it at that time.

Why, a man could get lost and die from starvation or snakebite or alligator attack or drowning and never be found, in those days.

This then was the area they chose in which to set up their stills and manufacture their booze. They knew the region well and appreciated its dangers and drawbacks as well as its advantages for their purpose. Absolutely inaccessible by foot, most of the land was marshy, so they had to set up light and easily movable stills which could be dismantled in a hurry and either cached under the dark brown water or hidden in the marsh grass and reeds. The operation was completely amphibious.

The undertaking went well at first. They were even closer to their sources of corn and other grains, which could be obtained by a short boat run. The locale was far enough away from even the villages of East Lake and Mashoes for smoke from the stills to be barely observable. The only access was by water and there was plenty of open space over the sound to spot any unfamiliar craft that might approach.

The quality controls that they had so rigorously followed were continued. Only the very purest stuff was to be made and no harmful diluents were allowed. There was no embalming fluid, no animal manure, no battery acid, nothing deleterious to hasten fermentation but ruin the purity of the product. The product was pure, if illegal, and its fame soon spread up and down the Atlantic seaboard. There was no delivery system. Customers had to come, usually by boat, to some designated rendezvous and pay cash for the merchandise which was usually sold in five gallon demijohns, complete with a large cork stopper and slatted protective crate. Purchase locations were changed frequently and rarely repeated.

Of course, this growing activity had to attract the attention of local, state, and federal forces charged with the enforcement of the unpopular prohibition laws. There was never any hint of collusion between the distillers and the local lawmen. The bootleggers knew the local lawmen and made it their business to watch them at all times. The operation was, indeed, a tough one to try to crack. The only approach to the region was by boat, and the moonshiners could always tell when an outsider was approaching in plenty of time to take appropriate action. Remember, these were family men, longtime residents of the coast and known and loved by most of the citizenry whether or not they approved of their activity. Clannish and close-knit, Bankers did not inform on another Banker, or at least you did not hear of it.

When the federal "Revenooers" began to move in, things began to heat up. They began to employ fast boats based nearby and the "shiners" retaliated by using even faster boats of their own. One man, who shall be known here only by his nickname of "Duck," even went so far as to construct a large barge upon which he mounted his still. Of extremely shallow draft and pushed by smaller boats, this floating distillery could be kept constantly on the move from one location to another to keep the agents completely confused.

The completed product was loaded into other fast, shallow-draft boats which dodged up and down East

Lake and South Lake and Deep Bay and even up the dead-end Northeast Prong. Some of the laden boats were dragged across the shallows at Haulover Point and thence down the shallow water of Durant's Island to Tom Mann Creek, where the depth of the water changed suddenly from fifteen feet to three feet with many underwater pilings to protect the knowledgeable boatman and exasperate a pursuer.

Thus there developed a sort of cat and mouse game of hide-and-seek with first one side winning and then the other. Gunfire was exchanged and there was some shedding of blood on both sides. Sometimes a boat loaded with liquor was captured but the crew usually escaped on foot through the marsh, braving the rattlesnakes and cottonmouths to remain unidentified.

Strangely, there developed a sort of mutual admiration between the "Revenooers" and their quarry. These men knew the moonshiners were not hardened criminals but otherwise honest fisher folk trying in the only way they knew to provide for their families. The bootleggers, for their part, realized that the agents were only men trying to do their job of enforcing an unpopular law.

It might have been this mutual regard or it might have been the heavy fogs that frequently occur but, although there were many rounds of gunfire exchanged, remarkably few wounds were suffered on either side. The catalyst came when a young man, making his first run with the "shiners," very foolishly stood up in his boat and was hit and seriously wounded. He had to be rushed by the federals' high-speed boat to a hospital where he almost died. This might have provoked a deadly escalation in the encounters but fortunately it did not work out that way.

No one pretends to know where or when any meeting occurred but surely there must have been a meeting of some kind. Local legend has it that shortly after the nearly fatal encounter, there was indeed such a meeting with some table pounding and rather violent language but it is believed that, in the end, they all departed peacefully with even some friendly farewells. Anyway, it is said that from that time on the cat and mouse game was continued with a difference. There was gunfire and there was pursuit, but most of the muzzle flashes streaked skyward and no more wounds were reported.

No actual capture of a fleeing booze-laden boat ever occurred but, strangely, about once every six weeks the federals would come upon a moored boat laden with moonshine in one of the canals. These craft were never found to be registered to anyone. They were mostly unseaworthy hulks on the verge of sinking but they were seized, as was the contraband on board.

Whether or not this is a true story, there was no more bloodshed and no one was ever killed. The seizing and destruction of large quantities of liquor put a rather severe crimp in the industry, which was gradually declining anyway. As times improved, more and more Bankers got out of the risky undertaking, but the fame of East Lake liquor remains to this day in the memory of old timers.

On December 5, 1933, the United States Congress adopted the Twenty-first Amendment to the Constitution of the United States. This effectively repealed the Eighteenth Amendment and put an end to a law that had never had complete public support. Long before that happened, the East Lake bootlegging business had gone the way of all outdated enterprises. What remains is the fact that although there were pitched battles of a sort, no one was ever killed. Although a few "shiners" were convicted and sentenced, they were usually allowed to pay large fines and endure probation. Thus, in what could have been a very ugly period of our history on the Outer Banks, no one was seriously prejudiced, all through a very practical expression of love and understanding among men unwilling to injure their fellow men.

Some of these men are still living and are good friends down to the present. This, too, can be credited to what is called the "East Lake accommodation."

The Magic Lute

THE LUTE IS AN ANCIENT MUSICAL instrument that is rarely, if ever, seen today except in music museums or possibly in some very comprehensive antique instrument shows. In the middle 1600s and for centuries before that, it was very popular. It was used then as a solo instrument or as an accompanying instrument for a solo vocalist. In ancient times it was used primarily to furnish a musical background for the recitation of poems or odes or even news or legends.

The *Encyclopedia Britannica* defines the lute as "an ancient stringed musical instrument, derived in form as well as name from the Arabs. . . . The Arab instrument, with convex sound body . . . was strung with silk . . . resembling the longitudinal section of a pear. As long as the strings were plucked by fingers or plectrum, the pear-shaped instrument may be identified as the archetype of the lute. . . . The lute was in general use during the 16th and 17th centuries. In the 18th it declined."

Dating back more than one thousand years, the lute was the instrument that replaced the lyre among the wandering musicians, entertainers, itinerant minstrels, and news bringers from the royal courts.

Our story takes place during the time when the lute was fading in popularity but was still enjoyed by many. It was still the more or less accepted form of entertainment for special occasions or feasts both in this country and in England.

In the middle 1600s the Outer Banks were beginning to be settled gradually by people moving down from southern Virginia and setting up households, both large and small, on the barrier strands of North Carolina. Some of these settlers were quite rich by the standards of that day and they established luxurious estates on the Banks.

No one questioned the sources of their wealth nor their reasons for choosing this isolated region to set up such elaborate establishments, but all enjoyed their hospitality. These settlers were mainly of English descent and their willingness to share with both neighbors and itinerant strangers was traditional and the expected norm. Visitors to such homesteads were not many, and they were usually greeted as welcome guests to help while away the occasional boredom on the isolated Banks. Visits in those days might last as little as a month or as long as several months.

One such family that settled in northern Currituck near Currituck Inlet was the Willingham family. Obviously people of some wealth, the family consisted of the father, Romulus Willingham, his son, Romulus, Jr., his wife, Marybell, and twin daughters, Susanna and Serena. These, plus an assortment of cooks, handymen, gardeners, and professional hunters made up the homestead.

Marybell ran the household and directed the servants, seeing to it that the freshly killed game brought in by the hunters was properly preserved and/or cured and tastefully served, that the fruits and vegetables produced by the gardeners were made to stretch far beyond the season of their ripening, and that the home was kept shiny clean. She also oversaw the entertainment of the guests in her home and secretly kept a sharp eye out for potential husbands for her twin girls.

Rom, Jr., was the "spittin' image" of his father. The son assisted in every possible way with the business end of maintaining the spread and generally made himself useful around the grounds. He was the idol of his sisters' eyes and was as spoiled and pampered as any twenty-one-year-old could possibly be. He seemed perfectly content to live the life of the country gentleman. He read extensively from his father's large library and thoroughly enjoyed the splendid hunting and fishing the region afforded. He was the perfect host when visitors were on hand, seeing to it that they were entertained and made comfortable during their stay.

The twins, a few years older than Rom, Jr., were just about as different from each other as they could well be.

They were not identical twins, either physically or personality-wise. Serena, the oldest by an hour, was a raven-haired beauty with piercing blue eyes and a somber, rather calculating attitude. Highly intelligent and perceptive, she was always the leader of the two, often getting the girls into typical childish scrapes when they were growing up. Susanna was the perfect foil of her sister. Blessed with an abundance of golden hair which fell below her shoulders, her soft brown eyes bespoke the gentle soul within. She was the sweet one of the pair. Always loving, always self-effacing, Susanna was usually the peacemaker in the family quarrels that occasionally arose. Both girls had long-limbed, well proportioned figures and the glowing beauty of youth and health. They were a pretty pair indeed, but, at age twenty-three they were approaching the age when women of that day were considered "maiden ladies" or, more bluntly, old maids.

Their mother was acutely aware of this and she secretly deplored the scarcity of suitable young men in the region who might qualify as suitors and potential husbands. She insisted on and arranged regular, chaperoned trips up to Jamestown, where both she and her girls thoroughly enjoyed the social life. The rounds of parties and soirees which seemed to go on continually provided ideal opportunity to meet people and to get to be known "in the right circles." They formed strong friendships with some of the wealthier settlers in Jamestown and often visited as houseguests for weeks on end while the young people celebrated and made merry in the ways young people always have and always will. It was a gentle, unhurried, and graceful time, and the inhabitants of the era knew how to make the most of it.

Social etiquette, of course, decreed that the Willinghams should act as hosts for return visits from these Jamestown friends. While the facilities for social activity were not as plentiful as in Jamestown, the Willinghams knew how to entertain and their guests were always anxious to return.

One such visitor was a highly eligible young bachelor named Rufus Durbeville. Young, handsome, and extremely fond of the outdoor life such as the Willinghams led, he was rumored to be of royal blood. Obviously wealthy, extremely well educated, and a thorough gentleman, he was welcome wherever he went.

Well, Rufus became "smitten" of both the twins and Marybell could not have been happier. She foresaw the marriage of this young man to one of her girls and she foresaw grandchildren and great-grandchildren to cheer her old age and perpetuate the family name. Wisely, she played strictly hands-off. Although she loved both her daughters, she would have no part in what was developing as a competition between them for the affections of young Rufus.

To begin with, the young man found them equally attractive and himself in the pleasant dilemma of choosing which one of the twins his heart preferred. As a guest in their home, he could not show partiality for either until the choice had been made. Gradually the sweetness and modesty of Susanna began to tilt his affections more and more in her direction. Finally, he approached Romulus,

Sr., with the request that he be given her hand in marriage. The father agreed, Susanna was also most willing, and so the engagement was announced. A wedding date some two months thence was agreed upon and preparation went forward for the wedding.

Joy reigned supreme in the Willingham household. Almost everyone was delighted that these two wonderfully suited young people were to be wed. Everyone, that is, except Serena. Hurt to the quick that the charms of her younger sister had been preferred to her own, she wept many bitter tears in the privacy of her bedroom. She could not blame Rufus. He had behaved with nothing but consideration for her in an attempt to ease her feelings. Serena seriously considered suicide, she was so hurt, but she dismissed that idea from her mind as being weak and unworthy of her. Instead, she began to cudgel her brain to see if she could devise some scheme whereby she could replace her sister and claim Rufus for her own. The sight of the two young people strolling arm in arm along the ocean strand, laughing and exchanging little confidences, was gall and wormwood to the jealous girl.

Now, this was the winter season on the Currituck Banks and the weather was, as it is today, frequently and unpredictably violent. The mighty Gulf Stream surged up from the south and the equally forceful but frigid Labrador Current streamed down from the north to violently collide just offshore. Sometimes one current and sometimes the other prevailed, and when the sea was stormy, these currents made it violent. Deep, swirling channels of water cut into the very shoreline. The weather after such a storm was usually beautiful with brilliant sunshine and fleecy clouds, but the sea would still be very dangerous with a swift current racing along the new channels cut near the shoreline.

The twins were used to taking winter strolls down to the ocean's edge when the weather was clearing to talk there and giggle together as sisters will. And thus it came to pass that on one sunny day after a storm, as they walked along the very edge of the bank above the swirling water, they talked of many things. Susanna's heart was full of joy and happiness as she talked of her approaching marriage and she told Serena that she wanted her to be maid of honor at the ceremony. To the older girl this was like pouring salt into an open wound and she inwardly writhed in torment with jealousy for her sister.

As they walked, the younger girl suddenly stumbled and slipped on the very edge of the storm-washed, eroded shore tumbling straight down toward the racing current just below the bank. Serena, ever alert and with quick reflexes, then pushed her sister down the steep slope and into the swift Labrador Current racing southward under a strong northeast wind. Susanna immediately found herself neck-deep in the cold, racing current.

"Help, Sister, help!" she cried in terror. Although a strong swimmer, she was no match for the surging current, and she felt herself weakening and being drawn under the icy waters. There was plenty of driftwood left by the storm on the beach but Serena made no effort to toss any of that to her drowning sister. With an evil smile, she sat herself down on the top of the slope and watched her sister lose a valiant fight against the cold and the force of the current. Still struggling but growing weaker and weaker, Susanna finally sank beneath the surface of the turbulent ocean and was seen no more.

Waiting until she deemed her sister to be irretrievably lost, the older twin ran to a shallow tide pool nearby and thoroughly soaked her dress up to the waist with sea water. Then she ran at full speed back to the homestead and, panting and sobbing, blurted out how her sister had stumbled and fallen into the tide. Still crying as though her heart would break, Serena then told how she, at the risk of her own life, had tried to save her but her own strength had given out and she had almost drowned with Susanna.

The community was shocked into immediate action. A thorough search was conducted all down the beach but there was no sign of the golden-haired girl. Small boats were even launched into the wild water but the search was to no avail. She was gone. Rufus was beside himself with grief. Night and day he mourned his lost love and roamed the deserted beach in the vain hope that he might yet find some sign, some clue that she had survived the icy grave. He lost all interest in hunting and fishing and scarcely ate enough to stay alive. At the insistence of young Romulus Willingham, he stayed on at the Willingham household in the forlorn hope that somehow, somehow she might have escaped. Romulus, Jr., was a tower of strength to him during his travail and treated him with genuine sympathy.

Serena, for her part, was the soul of compassion. She

comforted Rufus in any way she could. She even prepared little dishes of food she knew he liked to tempt
him into eating and becoming his former carefree self.
Of course, all this warm sympathy from a beautiful girl
and her more or less constant companionship began to
take effect. Serena was a very competent actress but she
didn't have to playact her affection for him. That was
genuine. He had always been fond of Serena, and now
this ripened into a genuine love on his part. Hesitantly
and after a long while, he proposed marriage. Serena, the
actress, played out her role to perfection. She feigned
indecision at accepting the hand of her dead sister's fi-
ancé, all the while confessing a sincere love for the
wealthy, young man. Of course, this was what she had
wanted all the while and she behaved modestly only to
conceal her jubilation at the success of her plan. She had
no remorse whatsoever for the death of her sister nor
for the part she had played in it.

Once again the young suitor called upon Romulus to
ask the hand of his daughter in marriage and, once again,
the father gave his consent. Marybell, with a woman's
intuition, often cast speculative glances toward her
daughter. It seemed to her that everything had happened just too perfectly for Serena and she knew all too
well her disposition and strongheadedness. But she had
no vestige of proof of any wrongdoing, so she kept her
peace but with many grave and troublesome doubts
about the forthcoming marriage.

Since it was so soon after Susanna's death, it was decided that the wedding festivities would be shortened.
What they were to lack in length Romulus decided

would be more than compensated by quality. While only a few of the closest Jamestown friends were invited, extra care was given to decorate the house and prepare much special food and drink. Romulus even sent two of his most trusted household servants far to the south to search for a minstrel who had become famous regionally. The servants were to hire the musician-storyteller to come and bring his entertainment to the nuptials.

Enter the lute.

A great distance to the south, near what is now the city of Wilmington, the pitiful body of Susanna had finally washed ashore. Preserved by the icy Labrador Current, she was nearly as beautiful and serene looking as she had been on the day she drowned. All the people were impressed with her beauty and especially with the long, golden tresses which spread below her waistline. They tried in vain to identify her. She had obviously been what they called a lady of quality and good taste and they hoped to be able to notify her family that she had been found. Communications were always poor in those days, particularly to isolated points.

The local people finally came to the conclusion that she had been lost overboard from some vessel at sea and they prepared to try to send word to the port authorities at Charleston in case her ship had docked there. Susanna was given a simple Christian burial in one of the family graveyards nearby and many prayers were offered in the cottages along the strand for the soul of one so young and so beautiful.

Now, at that winter season, a young minstrel named Overstreet had become weatherbound in his travels and had taken up residence with first one and then another of the local population. They welcomed him for the sweet songs he sang and for the beautiful melodies he played on his lute. This musical instrument was his passport into the homes and hearts of his hosts and he was a master of it.

He, too, had been on hand when the lovely body of Susanna was found on the shore, and he assisted with the preparations for the funeral. As were the rest, he was struck with the beauty of the girl and especially with the long, golden hair which encircled her head and shoulders like a halo. Now, it so happened that he had accidentally broken several of the silk strings on his lute and he did not know how to replace them. Overstreet asked the elders of the community if they thought there would be anything wrong with his taking several lengths of the silklike golden tresses to use to restring his lute. It was agreed that there could be no possible harm, so he reverently and gently cut several strands and used them soon thereafter to replace the broken and worn strings on his instrument. They gleamed on the lute like spun gold!

The substitution worked far beyond his expectations. From that day on, his lute began to play such beautiful and harmonious melodies and with such sweet and dulcet tones that his listeners were amazed. They likened the sounds to the music that must be made by the harps of the angels themselves. His fame quickly spread and his talents were suddenly in great demand. He decided then and there to tell no one of the source and nature of the strings on his lute. This was to be his secret and his great good fortune. He left the area soon thereafter and continued his travels toward Charleston.

Such was the situation when, in the late spring, the messengers of Romulus arrived in Charleston in their search for this accomplished musician and minstrel regardless of the cost. They were soon directed to Overstreet and the deal was made for the popular young performer to be present at the forthcoming wedding of Serena and Rufus.

So, several weeks before the scheduled wedding date, Overstreet showed up and was made most welcome by the Willingham household. The touch of this gifted entertainer was, they thought, just what was needed to brighten the atmosphere around the home and give a festive touch to the nuptials. Romulus had gone to considerable trouble and expense to obtain the talents of this entertainer, for he was determined that nothing should mar the wedding of his only remaining daughter.

Some two days after his arrival, the young minstrel agreed to give a preliminary rendition of his talents for the assembled wedding guests. It was spring but the weather was still a bit cool and a roaring fire glowed in the fireplace of the Willingham great room. All the candles and lamps had been extinguished, leaving only the flickering firelight. The houseguests, the betrothed pair, Marybell, Romulus, and Romulus, Jr., were assembled in anticipation of the beautiful music they had heard much about. Overstreet took his seat just outside the circle of firelight which played over the faces of the assembled throng and an expectant hush fell.

The minstrel had scarcely taken his lute out of its protective case when, to his amazement, the instrument began to play of its own accord without his touching the golden strings. Strangely, the sounds that poured forth from the lute were not those of a stringed instrument but the sweet voice of the drowned Susanna herself. The entire group sat transfixed, as the voice they knew so well came true and clear. Everyone, including the minstrel himself, was spellbound.

"Greeting to you, my sweet mother, Marybell," chimed the voice of the drowned girl. "Blessings be always upon you for the time and the care you spent rearing me and the unfailing love you always gave. Blessed be you, too, my honorable father and you, my younger brother."

"To you, Rufus, my betrothed, my beloved, thank you for the love you so gladly gave and for the life we could have had together," the voice continued. "May you find another love who will be worthy of you and who will make you happy your long life through. Be happy, my love, and please, once in a while, remember and think of your Susanna!"

Then the voice hardened. "To you, my unnatural sister, Serena, may you reap the harvest of your hate and jealousy and your willingness to kill to obtain your desires."

Then Susanna's voice proceeded to divulge each and every act that had led to her murder. The picture she painted of her killing hung like syllables of fire in the air before the hushed group.

As the lute fell silent, Serena leaped from her chair and, screaming, ran out of the house, down the long slope to the beach, and into the ocean. She disappeared under the waves and was never seen again. At least, her body was never found.

Once again, Rufus was heartbroken and in a state of shock. How much, he wondered, could a person stand? It seemed to him that the whole world was tumbling down around his head. The young man stayed on at the Willingham home while the search went on for Serena's body. He felt almost as though he was a member of the family after what he had been through. Finally, after all hope was abandoned, he packed up his things and went back to Jamestown. Some years later he married one of the colonial ladies and they moved back to Europe, where it is to be hoped that he finally found peace and happiness.

Marybell was grief-stricken at the swift and tragic turn of events and the sudden loss of both her daughters. Fortunately, one of the houseguests was a doctor and he was able to attend to her needs until she finally came out of shock. Romulus, Jr., did not marry but stayed with his parents until they both died and were buried in the little family plot back among the yaupon trees opposite Currituck Inlet. When they were both gone, he sold the homestead and migrated westward into the Province of Carolina where, it is said, he became a trapper and an Indian trader.

Henry Overstreet, the minstrel, left the homestead of the Willinghams a few days after Serena's tragedy. The news of the events spread up and down the coast and served to further enhance his fame and the demand for his services. The lute continued to play beautiful melodies in the hands of the troubadour, enchanting its listeners. But never again did it speak with the voice of a person, living or dead.

Within a few years the lute gradually became replaced with more modern instruments strung with catgut and metal strings, and the sweet voice of the golden strings was preserved only in the fond memory of the settlers on the Outer Banks. Down to this very day, in the quiet of a winter evening, they love to tell the story of the magic lute.

The Sea Angel

IN THE LATE SUMMER OF 1987, a young Dare County native who bears the given name of Freddie but who shall otherwise remain nameless here for privacy reasons was fishing his gill seine on the beach near Whalebone Junction. He set his net and left, returning about sundown to "haul" the net up on the beach. I walked down the beach to see what he had caught. Freddie welcomed me as a longtime family friend and told me he was expecting a large catch as all the signs were right and the weather was just about perfect.

The long net came in foot by foot, revealing a large catch of very good food-fish—trout, flounder, croaker, pompano, and perch, as well as the usual assortment of stingrays, skates, and small sand sharks. Freddie made me a present of two very fine speckled trout, refusing any payment for them. I thanked him and turned to make my way back up the beach to the cottage where I was staying when I noticed something unusual in the belly or "purse" of the net. The net was still in the wash of the gentle surf and inside that pouch the movement of a fairly large body of some kind was evident. Curious as to what it might be, I turned and walked cautiously down to the water's edge.

There, breathing heavily in the bight of the net, was a large, scaleless creature. It had large, prominent eyes and a snout resembling that of a pig. My first thought was that it must be a porpoise but I discarded that idea as I got closer and was able to see it more clearly. It was thrashing about heavily in the net and emitting little whistling sounds as though in great distress. As I walked even closer, I became aware that Freddie had left his fine catch of fish and was standing there beside me.

He started walking closer to the net and I asked, "Can I help you?" He replied, "No, thank you. I can manage." Wading out to the struggling creature, he tugged it free from the entangling mesh of the net. Seeing that it was too large for one man to carry and reassured by Freddie's touching the thing, I stepped in and took hold of the other seal-like flipper and immediately realized what it was. Together we then moved it out of the net and into knee-deep water. Pointing its head toward the open ocean, we released it and watched as it swam, turtle-like, into the deep water and disappeared under the gentle surf.

There in the fading light, Freddie and I stood in the

shallow water and just looked at each other for a long minute. Clearing his throat, he said simply, "Sea Angel." I nodded in silence, walked up onto the beach, picked up my trout, and headed cottageward. I had been privileged once again to see one of the rarest and most intriguing sights on our Outer Banks.

This was not the first Sea Angel I had seen and I hope it shall not be the last. It is not often that anyone now gets to see one. The experience triggered a childhood memory of one of the legends that few outsiders are privileged to hear but which make this golden beach so fascinating and mysterious. I felt humbled and awed as though I had been allowed to see for a brief moment into the days of long, long ago.

According to the seldom shared traditions of the true ancients of this region, the story of the Sea Angel begins a very long time ago. Its origin was some time between the disappearance of Sir Walter Raleigh's so-called Lost Colony and the beginnings of later recorded history in the region. The Outer Banks were being populated by a marvelous mixture of shipwreck survivors, immigrants from the sparsely settled country to the north, and travelers who, then as now, found the area irresistible. They survived by wringing a living from the sea in any way they could. It was a matter not of profit nor of accumulation of wealth but of survival in the face of bitter and frightening odds. Some were pirates, active and/or retired, others were boat builders or midwives or preachers or warlocks or witches, but all of them were wedded to the sea. Most of them were fishermen but all were survivors and pioneers in the finest sense.

One such was a middle-aged man named Esau. He lived a hermit-like existence in a little shack on the island of Portsmouth just across Ocracoke Inlet from the island of the same name. Where he came from or why no one knew and, Banker-like, they did not ask or pry. They knew only that he lived in his little dwelling on the waters of the sound just inside the inlet, that he fished almost daily in Pamlico Sound or in the ocean, and that he bothered no one. He was an excellent fisherman and his catch was usually a mixed bag of good, marketable fish, clams, crabs, oysters, and other seafood which brought a good price in Portsmouth Town.

His peers also knew that he was brave. Some of the other fishermen owed their lives to his courage and his expert seamanship, having been rescued by Esau from what otherwise would probably have been a tragic drowning. Extremely modest, he would probably have been embarrassed if anyone had called him a hero.

If this lonely man had a weakness, it was believed that it involved his fondness for strong drink upon occasion. When his catch was large enough, he sometimes bartered a part of it for a bottle or two of the rum that the local merchants imported from Jamaica. He never caused any trouble with this behavior. It was just somehow comforting when he had finished a hard day's work and returned to his humble shack, mended his nets, and gotten ready for the next day. On those occasions it was his custom to relax in the moonlight on the beach in front of his dwelling.

Lying on his back on the soft sand, he would feel the cooling breeze and gaze in wonder at the brilliant stars which seemed so close that he could almost reach up and touch them. If he fell asleep on the sand, what difference did it make? The nights were balmy and his sand-couch was comfortable and there was nothing there to harm him. If ever a hermit approached the perfect hermit life, that man was Esau.

It was on just such a starlit night that the hermit was awakened by the sounds of a violent thrashing about in the shallow waters just offshore. The frantic distress sounds of some creature in great affliction filled the air. Seizing an oar from his boat beached nearby, Esau dashed into the shallow water until he was waist deep in the sound. There, to his complete amazement, he beheld a large Mako shark circling the most beautiful mermaid you could imagine! Caught in the shallow water between the attacking shark and the shore, the mermaid had nowhere to go. If she attempted to gain the open water by swimming to either side of the attacking monster, it could easily circle in that direction and cut her off. Even though her superior speed would enable her to outdistance the shark in the open sea, he had the angle on her and she was trapped against the shore. Circling ever closer, the brute was narrowing the distance between himself and his prey.

Now Esau had never seen a mermaid but he had heard many tales about them from deepwater sailors and in his heart he believed implicitly in their existence. He had seen many things on the bosom of the ocean and in the waters of the sound that he could not explain by any logical rationale. He did not stop now to try to analyze this thing that was happening right before his eyes. Characteristically, he sprang immediately into action, heed-less of the danger to himself.

Surging by the distressed mermaid, he confronted the shark and began to beat it over the head with his heavy oar. The battle was on then and it might very well have ended tragically for Esau had the shark not been in shal-low water and had not the fisherman been a man of tre-mendous strength and courage. Digging his feet ankle deep in the sound bottom, he struck telling blows time after time as the shark attacked him. On one such sortie the creature bit off the blade of the hermit's oar, but Esau then used the jagged point that was left of the blade to stab the attacking creature in one of his gleaming eyes. Spouting blood from his blinded eye, the shark turned and disappeared into the deeper water of the sound, leaving a trail of blood behind him. Exhausted, the fisherman fell to his knees, released his broken oar to the falling tide, and crawled onto the beach. Totally spent from his battle, he dropped face down on the wet sand and lost consciousness.

When he came to his senses, the full moon was far down the western sky. The muscles in his arms and back ached terribly and his head throbbed as though it would split. He wondered if all that terrible fight had been just a bad dream or possibly the result of the bottle that lay empty beside him on the sand. He even questioned whether he was really losing his mind (becoming "loony") under the influence of that huge full moon now setting over the sound.

Suddenly he became aware that he was not alone. There on the beach beside him sat the beautiful mermaid, smiling and holding a handful of wet seaweed with which she had been bathing his fevered brow. That very moment marked the beginning of an entirely different period in the life of the hermit-fisherman. To his amazement and delight, he learned that she was indeed real flesh and blood, although of an entirely different nature from any other woman he had ever met. Her voice was soft and low and she spoke with a directness and sincerity that was charming. She was grateful for her rescue and sought ways to express her gratitude. A pleasant surprise was the discovery that they could talk and converse just like ordinary people, although Esau suspected that, if the truth were known, she could converse and be understood in any language.

She visited him often after that on his sandy beach and divulged many of the secrets of the sea. She could and did reveal to him the best times and places to fish and the best times to stay safe at home when the wild winds blew. Esau said nothing of this to his fellow humans. To begin with, he did not want them intruding on his new-found relationship, and he feared that they would think he had gone completely mad and would seek to spoil his recently discovered Eden.

Given the time and the location and his loneliness and her loveliness and gratitude, it was, perhaps, inevitable that they should fall in love. Being an honorable man, Esau proposed marriage to the beautiful creature from the sea. She was all in favor of the idea but tremendous difficulties immediately presented themselves. To begin with, they could think of no way to present themselves to the itinerant preacher who visited Portsmouth Island from time to time, even if they had been willing to wait that long, which they were not. If they should call upon the civil authorities for a ceremony, the nature of the mermaid would become immediately apparent. No, that was out of the question.

Finally they decided to call the creatures of nature as witnesses to their wedding: the sea gulls, the fiddler crabs, the porpoises, and the wild geese. They stood before the largest and oldest cypress tree on the island and, in the tradition of the Indians, declared themselves to be husband and wife.

The bride and groom had known from the very beginning that such an arrangement was against the basic law of the sea. Mermaids were supposed to lure sailors to their doom, not to permanent, ecstatic happiness. Mortals just did not marry mermaids. The few times in history that it had been tried had always ended in disaster. Stern punishment has been meted out to the few seafarers who, over the centuries, had been brash enough to defy that law. Poseidon, the king of the undersea, was known to be especially severe in his judgments. The newlyweds were desperately in love and, although they knew the risks of being discovered, they were blind to danger and rushed headlong into their marriage, hoping against hope that they could keep it concealed.

For a few weeks the world ran smoothly for the happy pair. Under his new wife's direction Esau became the most successful fisherman on the island. So much so that the others became very suspicious and reasoned that he must be in league with the devil. By plan she would spend most of her days visiting with other mermaids and her other friends of the undersea. Then, before sundown, she would make some excuse to absent herself and would swim happily to the deserted beach which she and Esau called home. The very secretiveness of their relationship loaned spice to their days and nights.

It was too perfect to last. No man ever achieves heaven on earth—at least not permanently. Thus it came about that on one beautiful, moonlit night Esau was awakened around midnight by the sound of a resonant, powerful bass voice calling his name. "Esau, Esau," the mighty voice boomed in tones that reverberated over the deserted beach, "come at once and do not delay. Poseidon, the mighty king of the sea, commands your presence in his court. Come at once!" Looking up, Esau beheld before him four ghosts of drowned seamen with wide, vacant stares and slack-jawed, open mouths. Their pallid, gray skins hung loosely on their bones and their hair hung down their backs in streaming disarray. It was the most terrible sight that Esau had ever seen and he struggled to get to his feet and run away into the sandhills.

Before he could regain his balance, he was seized in the icy grasp of those long-dead hands and forced to walk with them step by step out into the waters of the sound. Ever deeper and deeper they went until they vanished from sight and the calm waters closed over their heads. Scarcely a ripple disturbed the smooth waters at the spot where they disappeared. What route they took to Poseidon's court and exactly when they arrived will never be known. Arrive they did, though, and the court was organized to conduct the trial of Esau. Poseidon, in all his splendid robes bedecked with jewels from lost ships and a glittering crown that must have come from ancient Egypt, was the presiding judge.

For prosecutors the banshees were chosen. These were the wild, vengeful creatures who ride the winds of hurricanes with awful screams and who form the mighty maelstroms to suck great ships to their destruction. They were vigorous accusers. Over and over they demanded the most extreme punishment, citing the ancient law of the sea and the precedent of the severest punishment for sailors guilty of this crime.

Defending Esau were the naiads, the sea naiads, beautiful, gentle, and loving creatures, cousins to the mermaids themselves. They always tried to be helpful to all they met and were the exact opposites of the banshees. They defended Esau with urgent pleas for compassion and mercy. Very feminine and very eloquent, they cited his rescue of several fishermen, his honesty and good reputation, and his understandable yielding to the great love he felt for his mermaid.

The case was a sensation in the undersea world. All the creatures seemed to know about it and were fascinated with wonder as to what the king's decision would be. After the trial was over and after he had thought about the matter for some time, Poseidon called the fisherman before him and gave his decision. "Esau," the king said, "you have violated one of the most ancient laws of the sea. You deserve to be punished and you shall be punished, but I cannot overlook the pleas of the naiads and the many good things you have done for your fellow men.

"From this day forward and for all time," he continued, "you will not be allowed to return to your human world but will remain forever an undersea creature. You will be neither fish nor flesh but a creature shaped much like our turtles but without the turtle's protective shell. You shall not have scales like a fish but a fleshlike skin and fins. You shall spend eternity searching the sea for the troubled ghosts of seamen who have died at sea and are restless because they have not had a decent burial.

"You will be slow of speed and almost defenseless," Poseidon concluded, "but you will have my protection and any man or any creature who attempts to harm you will feel my wrath. If a human harms you, sharks will tear his nets and his family shall fall ill of various diseases and his boats shall spring leaks and founder. If it be a sea creature, he shall feel the weight of my wrath. On the other hand, if any human shall help you or assist you in any way, either by placing you back in the water when you are ashore or helping you in any other way, that human shall know the king's gratitude. His ventures, both at sea and on the shore, shall prosper and he and his family shall enjoy robust health and good luck."

Well, that is the story the ancients tell when you are lucky and/or trustworthy enough to get them to talk. I do not know what a Sea Angel is nor do I know its scientific title. I do know that they exist because I have seen them, not just once but a few times during my life. I have held one of them, or part of him, in my hands and have helped put him back in the sea to continue his search. And, yes, I cannot deny that I have been extremely lucky since that happened. I hope I meet him again.

A NOTE ON THE TYPE

The text of this book was set in a modern adaptation of Garamond, a typestyle designed by Claude Garamond, the foremost French type designer of the sixteenth century. The overall style is rounded, light and playful, but highly legible and simplistic in character.

Composed by
The Composing Room of Michigan, Inc.
Grand Rapids, Michigan

Manufactured by
R. R. Donnelley & Sons
Harrisonburg, Virginia